20 Recipes for Programming MVC 3

Jamie Munro

O'REILLY®

Beijing · Cambridge · Farnham · Köln · Sebastopol · Tokyo

20 Recipes for Programming MVC 3

by Jamie Munro

Published by O'Reilly Media, Inc., 1005 Gravenstein Highway North, Sebastopol, CA 95472.

O'Reilly books may be purchased for educational, business, or sales promotional use. Online editions are also available for most titles (*http://my.safaribooksonline.com*). For more information, contact our corporate/institutional sales department: (800) 998-9938 or *corporate@oreilly.com*.

Editors: Shawn Wallace and Mike Hendrickson

Production Editor: Kristen Borg

Proofreader: O'Reilly Production Services

Cover Designer: Karen Montgomery

Interior Designer: David Futato

Illustrator: Robert Romano

Revision History for the First Edition:

    2011-09-27   First release

See *http://oreilly.com/catalog/errata.csp?isbn=9781449309862* for release details.

ISBN: 978-1-449-30986-2

[LSI]

1317043391

To my wife and kids: you are a dream come true!

Table of Contents

Table of Contents

Preface

About The Book

The goal of a Model-View-Controller (MVC) framework is to allow developers to easily separate their code in distinct aspects to simplify development tasks. The model layer allows us to integrate with data; usually a database table. The view layer allows us to represent our data in a visual fashion using a combination of HTML and CSS. The controller layer is the middleman between the model and view. The controller is used to retrieve data from a model and make that data available for a view.

The goal of this book is to provide web developers a cookbook of "recipes" that are required by many developers on a day-to-day basis. Each code sample contains a complete working example of how to implement authentication, email, AJAX, data validation, and many other examples. You will quickly find yourself referring to one of these samples for every website that you build.

Prerequisites

Before beginning with this book, it is important to have a good understanding of web development. This book is heavily focused on providing useful code samples. Each code sample is well described; however, it is assumed that the reader is already familiar with many aspects of web development.

I would highly recommend reviewing ASP.NET's MVC (*http://www.asp.net/mvc*) website before starting. Within a few quick minutes you will be up-to-speed and ready to go—it's that easy.

Conventions Used in This Book

The following typographical conventions are used in this book:

Italic

> Indicates new terms, URLs, email addresses, filenames, and file extensions.

`Constant width`

> Used for program listings, as well as within paragraphs to refer to program elements such as variable or function names, databases, data types, environment variables, statements, and keywords.

`Constant width bold`

> Shows commands or other text that should be typed literally by the user.

`Constant width italic`

> Shows text that should be replaced with user-supplied values or by values determined by context.

> This icon signifies a tip, suggestion, or general note.

> This icon indicates a warning or caution.

Tools

There are many Integrated Development Environments (IDEs) available on the Internet. I have several favorites; one for each language that I develop in. For example, if I'm developing in PHP, I really like PHPStorm by Jet Brains. When I'm developing in .NET, there is only one clear choice: Microsoft Visual Studio.

If you are an individual just looking to get started, I would recommend the express edition: *http://www.microsoft.com/express/Downloads/*. It's available for free, you simply need to register within 30 days of use. I would also suggest that you download and install SQL Server 2008 R2 Express as well.

Visual Studio Developer Express will allow us to create and maintain our projects, while SQL Server Express will allow us to create and maintain our databases. All rich Internet applications these days contain a database of some sort to store data captured from user input.

At the time of writing this book, the current version of Visual Studio does not contain MVC 3 templates by default. These need to be downloaded before you begin. Visit ASP.NET's MVC (*http://www.asp.net/mvc*) web page to download and install it.

Using Code Examples

This book is here to help you get your job done. In general, you may use the code in this book in your programs and documentation. You do not need to contact us for permission unless you're reproducing a significant portion of the code. For example, writing a program that uses several chunks of code from this book does not require permission. Selling or distributing a CD-ROM of examples from O'Reilly books does require permission. Answering a question by citing this book and quoting example code does not require permission. Incorporating a significant amount of example code from this book into your product's documentation does require permission.

Not all code is optimized for best performance or error handling. Regions are used throughout the examples to allow the code to be suppressed in future examples. Partial views are used as well to help separate the code between recipes and focus more on the changes.

 All code, data and examples can be downloaded from our the book's web page at *http://www.oreilly.com/catalog/0636920021407*.

We appreciate, but do not require, attribution. An attribution usually includes the title, author, publisher, and ISBN. For example: "*20 Recipes for Programming MVC 3* by Jamie Munro (O'Reilly). Copyright 2011 Jamie Munro, 978-1-449-30986-2."

If you feel your use of code examples falls outside fair use or the permission given above, feel free to contact us at *permissions@oreilly.com*.

Safari® Books Online

 Safari Books Online is an on-demand digital library that lets you easily search over 7,500 technology and creative reference books and videos to find the answers you need quickly.

With a subscription, you can read any page and watch any video from our library online. Read books on your cell phone and mobile devices. Access new titles before they are available for print, and get exclusive access to manuscripts in development and post feedback for the authors. Copy and paste code samples, organize your favorites, download chapters, bookmark key sections, create notes, print out pages, and benefit from tons of other time-saving features.

O'Reilly Media has uploaded this book to the Safari Books Online service. To have full digital access to this book and others on similar topics from O'Reilly and other publishers, sign up for free at *http://my.safaribooksonline.com*.

How to Contact Us

Please address comments and questions concerning this book to the publisher:

O'Reilly Media, Inc.
1005 Gravenstein Highway North
Sebastopol, CA 95472
800-998-9938 (in the United States or Canada)
707-829-0515 (international or local)
707-829-0104 (fax)

We have a web page for this book, where we list errata, examples, and any additional information. You can access this page at:

http://www.oreilly.com/catalog/0636920021407/

To comment or ask technical questions about this book, send email to:

bookquestions@oreilly.com

For more information about our books, courses, conferences, and news, see our website at *http://www.oreilly.com*.

Find us on Facebook: *http://facebook.com/oreilly*

Follow us on Twitter: *http://twitter.com/oreillymedia*

Watch us on YouTube: *http://www.youtube.com/oreillymedia*

The Recipes

1.1 Restricting Access to Views with Password Protection

Problem

You want to prevent access to specific pages of your website unless a user has registered and logged in with a username and password.

Solution

Implement ASP.NET's `AuthorizeAttribute`, `FormsAuthentication`, and `Membership` creation/validation through the use of an `AccountController`, `AccountModels`, and several MVC views.

Discussion

The MVC team at Microsoft have made a lot of improvements to the `AccountController`. It has been updated to use `FormsAuthentication` along with the `Membership` class to create new users, validate existing users, and create cookies to check the logged in state of users.

Unlike MVC 2, in version 3, the new project dialog has been updated to provide several different start up applications: *Empty*, *Internet Application*, and *Intranet Application*. An empty application will set up your folder structure required for MVC. An *Internet Application*, the default template, will create an MVC application with several features pre-configured, including a basic layout and an `AccountController` that contains multiple actions to register and log users the application. The third template, *Intranet Application*, is quite similar to the Internet Application with the exception that instead of using the `Membership` class, it will use Windows Authentication.

For most websites, the default *Internet Application* should be used. If you haven't already done so, create a new MVC 3 Internet Application now. This will generate an `AccountController`, `AccountModels`, and several Account views that contain forms for users to register, log in, and change their password with.

It is important to note the name of your new MVC application. Throughout the examples in this book, the namespace will be Mvc Application4. If your application name is different, all of the namespaces in the subsequent examples must be updated to reflect your namespace.

To prevent users from accessing certain views, MVC provides an AuthorizeAttribute that is placed in a controller above the action requiring the user to be logged in to view the particular content. Open the AccountController and you will see that this is done here:

```
//
// GET: /Account/ChangePassword

[Authorize]
public ActionResult ChangePassword()
{
    return View();
}
```

When a user attempts to access the page /Account/ChangePassword, if they have not previously logged in or registered on your website, MVC will automatically redirect them to the login page. If they have already logged in, no redirect will take place and the view will be displayed to them. The URL that the user is redirected to when not logged in is defined in the Web.config file here:

```
<authentication mode="Forms">
  <forms loginUrl="~/Account/LogOn" timeout="2880" />
</authentication>
```

If the user has never registered before, they will end up at the registration page. The default registration collects the following information:

- Username
- Email Address
- Password

The functionality that creates a new Membership for the user is completed inside the AccountController in the Register function. The Register function accepts one parameter called model that is of type RegisterModel. In the AccountModels, there is a class definition called RegisterModel that defines public variables for each of the form elements on the register page.

It's important to ensure that every time a model is being posted through a form that one of the first conditional checks is for Model State.IsValid. In a future example, when validation is implemented, this boolean field verifies that the data entered through the form is valid data and matches the model definition.

```
[HttpPost]
public ActionResult Register(RegisterModel model)
{
    if (ModelState.IsValid)
    {
        // Attempt to register the user
        MembershipCreateStatus createStatus;
        Membership.CreateUser(model.UserName,
            model.Password, model.Email, null, null,
                true, null, out createStatus);

        if (createStatus ==
                MembershipCreateStatus.Success)
        {
            FormsAuthentication.SetAuthCookie(
                model.UserName,
                false /* createPersistentCookie */);
            return RedirectToAction("Index", "Home");
        }
        else
        {
            ModelState.AddModelError("",
                ErrorCodeToString(createStatus));
        }
    }

    // If we got this far, something failed,
    // redisplay form
    return View(model);
}
```

The above code was generated automatically, and does three important things:

1. Creates a new user through the `Membership.CreateUser()` function with the data that was entered by the user.

2. Ensures that the user was successfully created, and if so, a `FormsAuthentica tion.SetAuthCookie` is set that is used to validate the user on subsequent page calls.

3. If the user was created successfully, the user is redirected back to the homepage (or if there was an error creating the user, an error message is set and passed to the view and is redisplayed with an error message to the user).

If you have installed the full version of Visual Studio, SQL Express is also installed allowing you to view your databases that are created. However, if you have only installed the basic version of Visual Studio, SQL Express can be downloaded from Microsoft for free as well.

The default database connection defined in the Web.config will create a SQL Express database in the `App_Data` folder of the application. This local SQL Express database will contain the various tables required by the *Membership* class to store the users, profile data, roles, etc., for the application.

```
<connectionStrings>
  <add name="ApplicationServices"
      connectionString="data source=.\SQLEXPRESS;
         Integrated Security=SSPI;
         AttachDBFilename=|DataDirectory|aspnetdb.mdf;
         User Instance=true"
         providerName="System.Data.SqlClient" />
</connectionStrings>
```

When a user visits the website again in the future, if the FormsAuthentication cookie is still present (because they chose the "remember me" option during login—or they didn't close their web browser) then the content will be displayed to them without being required to log in or register. However, if the cookie isn't present, but the user has already registered, they will be redirected to the login page. Once the user enters their login information and submits the form, the AccountController will once again handle the processing to validate the user through the Membership class. This is shown here:

```
[HttpPost]
public ActionResult LogOn(LogOnModel model,
        string returnUrl)
{
    if (ModelState.IsValid)
    {
        if (Membership.ValidateUser(model.UserName,
            model.Password))
        {
            FormsAuthentication.SetAuthCookie(
                model.UserName, model.RememberMe);
            if (Url.IsLocalUrl(returnUrl)
                && returnUrl.Length > 1
                    && returnUrl.StartsWith("/")
                && !returnUrl.StartsWith("//")
                    && !returnUrl.StartsWith("/\\"))
            {
                return Redirect(returnUrl);
            }
            else
            {
                return RedirectToAction("Index", "Home");
            }
        }
        else
        {
            ModelState.AddModelError("",
                "The user name or password provided
                is incorrect.");
        }
    }

    // If we got this far, something failed,
    // redisplay form
    return View(model);
}
```

The above code, once again automatically generated, does three important things:

1. Validates the user through the `Membership.ValidateUser()` function with the user-name and password entered.
2. If the login was successful, a `FormsAuthentication.SetAuthCookie` is set.
3. If the user was validated, the user is redirected back to the homepage (or if they were not validated, an error message is set and passed to the view that is redisplayed with an error message to the user).

The `AuthorizeAttribute` also provides further restriction options by limiting pages to certain groups or even only certain users. This can be accomplished as follows:

```
// Retrieve a list of all users to allow an admin
// to manage them
[Authorize(Roles = "Admin")]
public ActionResult UserAdmin()
{
    MembershipUserCollection users =
        Membership.GetAllUsers();
    return View(users);
}

// Create some custom reports for me only
[Authorize(Users = "Jamie")]
public ActionResult JamieAdmin()
{
    // Perform some logic to generate usage reports
    ...
    return View();
}
```

These simple examples are merely the beginning of how content can be restricted. Some next steps would be to consider exploring adding custom groups to further advance the definition of the access control.

See Also

AuthorizeAttribute (*http://msdn.microsoft.com/en-us/library/system.web.mvc.authorizeattribute.aspx*), FormsAuthentication (*http://msdn.microsoft.com/en-us/library/system.web.security.formsauthentication.aspx*), and Membership (*http://msdn.microsoft.com/en-us/library/system.web.security.membership.aspx*)

1.2 Automating Generation of Controllers and Views

Problem

You want to allow dynamic content to be managed through your website.

Solution

Automatically generate a controller and multiple views through scaffolding allowing users to Create, Read, Update, and Delete (also known as CRUD) data with the *Entity Framework Code-First* and *Database-First* approaches.

Discussion

Before the controller and views can be scaffolded, a model and DbContext need to be created that define what data is to be collected (hence the *Code-First* approach). In the following example, two classes are created that will provide the ability to manage a list of books. The first class contains the definition of the book data that will be stored in the SQL Express database. The second class contains the DbContext that creates a DbSet of the Book class. To create the model, right click on the Models folder and select *Add→Class*. In the filename field type: Book.cs and replace the generated class with the following code:

```
using System;
using System.Collections.Generic;
using System.Linq;
using System.Web;
using System.Data.Entity;

namespace MvcApplication4.Models
{
    public class Book
    {
        public int ID { get; set; }
        public string Title { get; set; }
        public string Isbn { get; set; }
        public string Summary { get; set; }
        public string Author { get; set; }
        public string Thumbnail { get; set; }
        public double Price { get; set; }
        public DateTime Published { get; set; }
    }

    public class BookDBContext : DbContext
    {
        public DbSet<Book> Books { get; set; }
    }
}
```

With the Book model and BookDBContext created, the scaffolding of the controller and view can now be completed. To begin, right click on the Controllers folder and select *Add→Controller* (see Figure 1-1).

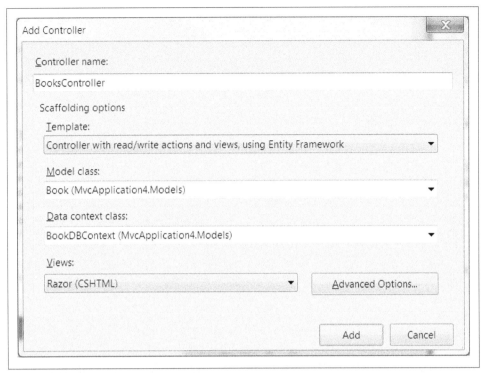

Figure 1-1. Adding a new controller

 People have different naming conventions for controllers. As much as possible, I attempt to use a plural name for my controller and a singular name for my model classes. The reasoning behind this is the controller provides the ability to view, add, edit, and delete one or more books; while the model pertains to a single book record.

As you can see in the above picture, the new controller is named BooksController. From the template dropdown, choose a controller with read/write actions and views, using the Entity Framework. The model class is the previously created Book class and the Data context class is the previously created BookDBContext class. Razor is the default type for the views, so this can be left as-is. Once you have filled out and entered the correct information, press *Add* and wait several seconds as the files are created (see Figure 1-2).

 If you see an error underneath the model class indicating no models can be found, try building or running the solution first, then try again.

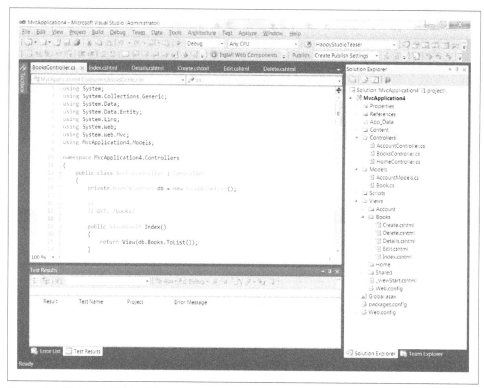

Figure 1-2. Newly scaffolded files

The *Entity Framework* also provides the ability to scaffold controllers and views by using a different method, *Database-First*. This is done by creating an Entity Data Model to an already existing database. In large projects, it is quite common to separate based on the strength of the resources available. For example, a good front-end web developer might not be an expert at database design. So the task of designing a database will be given to an expert.

In the next example, a connection to the previously created database containing the Books table will be created and scaffolded from that instead of a model. Begin by creating a new application. The old application can be used again, but creating a new application will allow you to decide your preference for creating models, *Code-First* or *Database-First*.

Once the application is created, right click on the Models folder and select *Add→New Item*. In the search box in the top right corner, type Entity. From the search results, select *ADO.NET Entity Data Model*. Update the name of the file to be BookModel .edmx. Now it's time to go through a wizard to set up the database connection:

1. Select Generate from database.
2. Select the New connection button.
3. Select Microsoft SQL Server from the drop-down and press Continue.
4. In the Connection Properties dialog, under Server Name, select your SQL Express database.
5. Under the Connect to a database drop-down, select the database that was automatically created by MVC in the last example and press OK.

Update the connection string for Web.config to be SQLExpressConnection and press Next. A connection will be now made to the database. Expand the Tables and select the Books table.

After selecting Finish, the new Entity Diagram is created under the Models directory. Before the controller can be scaffolded, the solution must be built. Once the project is built, just like in the *Code-First* example, right click on the Controllers folder and select *Add→Controller*.

When adding the new controller in this approach, the Book is still the Model class; however, for the Data context class, Entities is chosen instead which contains the connection to the database.

In future recipes, the *Code-First* approach will be used to allow for more complete code examples instead of requiring database tables to be manually created and allow for more focus on MVC.

See Also

ADO.NET Entity Framework Overview (*http://msdn.microsoft.com/en-us/library/ aa697427(v=vs.80).aspx*)

1.3 Validating User Input

Problem

You need to ensure that the data being captured in your form contains the data expected based on your database or model design.

Solution

.NET 4.0 contains a new `DataAnnotations` namespace that provides many useful metadata attribute classes that have been implemented in MVC 3. For the purpose of validating form input the following attribute classes can be used to provide a wide variety of validation options: `RequiredAttribute`, `RegularExpressionAttribute`, `RangeAttribute`, and `DataTypeAttribute`. When custom validation is required, MVC 3 also supports the improvements to the `ValidationAttribute` class allowing developer-defined validation.

Discussion

The following example is going to extend the *Code-First Book* model that was created in the previous recipe. It will be updated to ensure the following:

1. A book title is entered.
2. A valid ISBN is entered.
3. A book summary is entered.
4. An author of the book is entered.
5. A valid dollar amount for the price of the book is entered.
6. A valid published date is entered.

Five of the six validation requirements can be met with the built-in validation methods provided with MVC 3. The ISBN validation; however, needs to be done in a different format—it requires a custom validation method:

```
using System;
using System.Collections.Generic;
using System.Linq;
using System.Web;
using System.Data.Entity;
using System.ComponentModel.DataAnnotations;
using MvcApplication4.Validations;

namespace MvcApplication4.Models
{
    public class Book
    {
        public int ID { get; set; }

        [Required]
        public string Title { get; set; }

        [Required]
        [IsbnValidation]
        public string Isbn { get; set; }

        [Required]
        public string Summary { get; set; }
```

```
        [Required]
        public string Author { get; set; }

        public string Thumbnail { get; set; }

        [Range(1, 100)]
        public double Price { get; set; }

        [DataType(DataType.Date)]
        [Required]
        public DateTime Published { get; set; }
    }

    public class BookDBContext : DbContext
    {
        public DbSet<Book> Books { get; set; }
    }
}
```

In the above example, the [Required] data annotation was added above each field that must be provided by the user. Above the ISBN number, [IsbnValidation] was also added, informing MVC 3 that it must call the IsValid operation from the soon-to-be created IsbnValidationAttribute class. To validate the price, the [Range] annotation was used. This could also be accomplished with the [RegularExpression] attribute as follows:

```
[RegularExpression (@"(\b[\d\.]*)")]
public double Price { get; set; }
```

Finally, the published date is validated by telling MVC that the DataType of this field is a date. The IsbnValidation data attribute will currently be displaying an error because this class has not been implemented. This class will be implemented in the following example.

A valid ISBN is defined as 10 or 13 characters long. To help keep the code organized, the custom validation will be placed in a separate folder where other custom validation that might be needed can be added as well. Right click on the project and select *Add→New Folder*. The folder should be named Validations. Once created, right click on the new folder and select *Add→Class*. Name the class IsbnValidationAttribute.cs. This class will extend the *ValidationAttribute* class and override the IsValid method to perform validation on the ISBN number entered:

```
using System;
using System.Collections.Generic;
using System.Linq;
using System.Web;
using System.Text.RegularExpressions;

namespace MvcApplication4.Validations
{
    [AttributeUsage(AttributeTargets.Field |
        AttributeTargets.Property, AllowMultiple = false,
            Inherited = true)]
```

```csharp
public class IsbnValidationAttribute :
    System.ComponentModel.DataAnnotations.ValidationAttribute
{
    /**
     * This class is courtesy:
     * http://www.java2s.com/Open-Source/CSharp/
     * Inversion-of-Control-Dependency-Injection/Spring.net/
     * Spring/Validation/Validators/ISBNValidator.cs.htm
     *
     * This class is used for demonstration purposes
     * of performing an ISBN validation.  Should you
     * wish to use this in your project, please
     * consult the license agreement here:
     * http://www.apache.org/licenses/LICENSE-2.0
     **/

    private static readonly String SEP = "(?:\\-|\\s)";
    private static readonly String GROUP = "(\\d{1,5})";
    private static readonly String PUBLISHER = "(\\d{1,7})";
    private static readonly String TITLE = "(\\d{1,6})";

    static readonly String ISBN10_PATTERN =
        "^(?:(\\d{9}[0-9X])|(?:" + GROUP + SEP + PUBLISHER +
            SEP + TITLE + SEP + "([0-9X])))$";

    static readonly String ISBN13_PATTERN =
        "^(978|979)(?:(\\d{10})|(?:" + SEP + GROUP + SEP +
            PUBLISHER + SEP + TITLE + SEP + "([0-9])))$";

    public IsbnValidationAttribute() :
        base("Invalid ISBN number")
    {
    }

    public override bool IsValid(object value)
    {
        // Convert to string and fix up the ISBN
        string isbn = value.ToString();
        string code = (isbn == null)
          ? null :
            isbn.Trim().Replace("-", "").Replace(" ", "");

        // check the length
        if ((code == null) || (code.Length < 10
                || code.Length > 13))
        {
            return false;
        }

        // validate/reformat using regular expression
        Match match;
        String pattern;
        if (code.Length == 10)
        {
```

```
                pattern = ISBN10_PATTERN;
            }
            else
            {
                pattern = ISBN13_PATTERN;
            }

            match = Regex.Match(code, pattern);
            return match.Success && match.Index == 0 &&
                match.Length == code.Length;
        }
    }
}
```

The above example contains a standard ISBN validation check provided as a demonstration from the CSharp Open Source example (*http://www.java2s.com/Open-Source/CSharp/Inversion-of-Control-Dependency-Injection/Spring.net/Spring/Validation/Validators/ISBNValidator.cs.htm*). If the ISBN matches one of the two regular expression patterns, the IsValid function will return true; otherwise, it will return false, requiring the user to try again.

If you go to the book's create page in your web browser, when you press Submit, the above error messages will appear until the form contains valid data. As you may recall in the first recipe, this is done by checking that the ModelState.IsValid is equal to true.

See Also

DataAnnotations Namespace (*http://msdn.microsoft.com/en-us/library/system.componentmodel.dataannotations.aspx*)

1.4 Implementing Multiple Languages

Problem

The Internet is used by millions of people in hundreds of different countries and hundreds of different languages; even English has multiple different dialects between Canada, USA, and Great Britain. It is important to not limit the exposure of your website by only offering your website in one language.

Solution

Create resource files and add all of the static text as key/value pairs and implement the CurrentUICulture to provide the ability to change languages.

Discussion

Resource files are text-based XML files that are used to make static websites support multiple languages. You create a main resource file that contains your default language.

Then everywhere that text is stored in your controllers, models, or views, you create a key/value pair for the text. Figure 1-3 shows an example resource file.

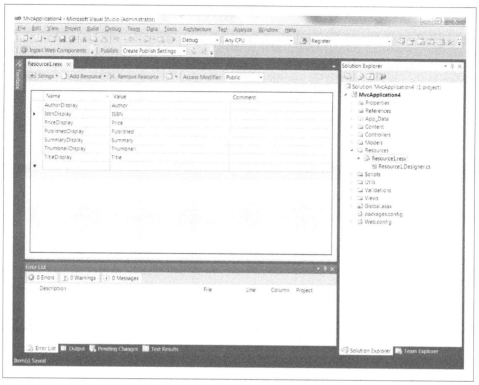

Figure 1-3. Sample resource file

 When you create a resource file, in the top-right corner make sure that the *Access Modifier* is set to `Public` instead of the default `No code gener ation`. MVC won't be able to access the file if it is not public.

To create your resource file, begin by right-clicking your MVC application and select *Add→New Folder*. Call the new folder `Resources`. With the new folder selected, right-click and select *Add→New Item*. In the search type *resource* and select the Resources File.

As you can see in the above example, I have created one entry per field in the Book model class. The next step is to update the model to reference these values in the `DisplayAttribute`:

```
using System;
using System.Collections.Generic;
using System.Linq;
using System.Web;
```

```
using System.Data.Entity;
using System.ComponentModel.DataAnnotations;
using MvcApplication4.Validations;

namespace MvcApplication4.Models
{
    public class Book
    {
        public int ID { get; set; }

        [Required]
        [Display(Name = "TitleDisplay",
            ResourceType = typeof(Resources.Resource1))]
        public string Title { get; set; }

        [Display(Name = "IsbnDisplay",
            ResourceType = typeof(Resources.Resource1))]
        [Required]
        [IsbnValidation]
        public string Isbn { get; set; }

        [Display(Name = "SummaryDisplay",
            ResourceType = typeof(Resources.Resource1))]
        [Required]
        public string Summary { get; set; }

        [Display(Name = "AuthorDisplay",
            ResourceType = typeof(Resources.Resource1))]
        [Required]
        public string Author { get; set; }

        [Display(Name = "ThumbnailDisplay",
            ResourceType = typeof(Resources.Resource1))]
        public string Thumbnail { get; set; }

        [Display(Name = "PriceDisplay",
            ResourceType = typeof(Resources.Resource1))]
        [Range(1, 100)]
        public double Price { get; set; }

        [Display(Name = "PublishedDisplay",
            ResourceType = typeof(Resources.Resource1))]
        [DataType(DataType.Date)]
        [Required]
        public DateTime Published { get; set; }
    }

    public class BookDBContext : DbContext
    {
        public DbSet<Book> Books { get; set; }
    }
}
```

In the above example, the `DisplayAttribute` is used to retrieve the key from the resource file by specifying the key in the name field and the resource file in the resource type. A similar process must be completed for each view and controller.

 To help make debugging resource files easier and avoid processing data within a view, I suggest setting `ViewBag` variables in a controller and referencing these values in the view. It is possible to access the resource file directly from a view; however, views are not compiled by Visual Studio and you will receive a run-time error if you make a mistake. Whereas if you place the resource access in the controller, Visual Studio will display an error if the specified resource key is not found.

The following example will update the Books Index view to move the static text to the resource file. If you examine the index view, there are not a lot of items that need to be moved to the resource file. Create the key/value pairs shown in Table 1-1.

Table 1-1. Resource file updates

Key	Value
BookIndexTitle	Index
CreateLink	Create New
EditLink	Edit
DetailsLink	Details
DeleteLink	Delete

Since only one resource file is being created, all keys must be unique to the entire project. As you can see, I have made the bottom four keys quite generic, as these can be used by all future views that contain these links.

Once the resource file updates have been completed, open the `BooksController` and replace the `Index()` function with the following:

```
//
// GET: /Books/

public ViewResult Index()
{
    #region ViewBag Resources
    ViewBag.Title =
        Resources.Resource1.BookIndexTitle;
    ViewBag.CreateLink =
        Resources.Resource1.CreateLink;
    ViewBag.TitleDisplay =
        Resources.Resource1.TitleDisplay;
    ViewBag.IsbnDisplay =
        Resources.Resource1.IsbnDisplay;
    ViewBag.SummaryDisplay =
        Resources.Resource1.SummaryDisplay;
```

```
        ViewBag.AuthorDisplay =
            Resources.Resource1.AuthorDisplay;
        ViewBag.ThumbnailDisplay =
            Resources.Resource1.ThumbnailDisplay;
        ViewBag.PriceDisplay =
            Resources.Resource1.PriceDisplay;
        ViewBag.PublishedDisplay =
            Resources.Resource1.PublishedDisplay;
        ViewBag.EditLink =
            Resources.Resource1.EditLink;
        ViewBag.DetailsLink =
            Resources.Resource1.DetailsLink;
        ViewBag.DeleteLink =
            Resources.Resource1.DeleteLink;
        #endregion

        return View(db.Books.ToList());
    }
```

 In the above code example, a #region tag named ViewBag Resources has been added around all of the variables. In future examples, this region will be hidden to help provide focus on any new code being added to the BooksController.

Finally the Books Index view must be updated to reference these ViewBag properties instead of the static text that was previously there:

```
@model IEnumerable<MvcApplication6.Models.Book>

<h2>@ViewBag.Title</h2>

<p>
    @Html.ActionLink((string)ViewBag.CreateLink, "Create")
</p>
<table>
    <tr>
        <th>
            @ViewBag.TitleDisplay
        </th>
        <th>
            @ViewBag.IsbnDisplay
        </th>
        <th>
            @ViewBag.SummaryDisplay
        </th>
        <th>
            @ViewBag.AuthorDisplay
        </th>
        <th>
            @ViewBag.ThumbnailDisplay
        </th>
```

```
        <th>
            @ViewBag.PriceDisplay
        </th>
        <th>
            @ViewBag.PublishedDisplay
        </th>
        <th></th>
    </tr>

@foreach (var item in Model) {
    <tr>
        <td>
            @Html.DisplayFor(modelItem => item.Title)
        </td>
        <td>
            @Html.DisplayFor(modelItem => item.Isbn)
        </td>
        <td>
            @Html.DisplayFor(modelItem => item.Summary)
        </td>
        <td>
            @Html.DisplayFor(modelItem => item.Author)
        </td>
        <td>
            @Html.DisplayFor(modelItem => item.Thumbnail)
        </td>
        <td>
            @Html.DisplayFor(modelItem => item.Price)
        </td>
        <td>
            @Html.DisplayFor(modelItem => item.Published)
        </td>
        <td>
            @Html.ActionLink((string)ViewBag.EditLink,
                "Edit", new { id=item.ID }) |
            @Html.ActionLink((string)ViewBag.DetailsLink,
                "Details", new { id = item.ID }) |
            @Html.ActionLink((string)ViewBag.DeleteLink,
                "Delete", new { id = item.ID })
        </td>
    </tr>
}

</table>
```

This same logic should be completed for the remaining views and controller actions as well. Once all views and actions have been updated, the resource file must be duplicated into another language.

To avoid extra typing, I would suggest waiting to do this process until all of the text has been added to your resource file. With the main resource file selected, right-click it and select Copy. Then select the *Resources* folder, right-click, and choose Paste. This file then must be renamed as Resources1.fr.resx. Replace Resources1 with the name of your main resource file and rename fr with the language you wish to set up. This file can be then sent to a translator and updated by the translator to replace the English text with the appropriate wording in the other language.

To perform the language change, the `Global.asax.cs` file must be updated to change the `CurrentUICulture` for each request that occurs. This can be done by adding the following code to the `Application_AcquireRequestState()` function:

```
using System;
using System.Collections.Generic;
using System.Linq;
using System.Web;
using System.Web.Mvc;
using System.Web.Routing;
using MvcApplication4.Models;
using System.Data.Entity;
using System.Globalization;
using System.Threading;

namespace MvcApplication4
{

    public class MvcApplication : System.Web.HttpApplication
    {
        ...

        protected void Application_AcquireRequestState(
            object sender, EventArgs e)
        {
            if (HttpContext.Current.Session != null)
            {
                CultureInfo ci =
                    (CultureInfo)this.Session["CurrentLanguage"];
                if (ci == null)
                {
                    ci = new CultureInfo("en");
                    this.Session["CurrentLanguage"] = ci;
                }

                Thread.CurrentThread.CurrentUICulture = ci;
                Thread.CurrentThread.CurrentCulture =
                    CultureInfo.CreateSpecificCulture(ci.Name);
            }
        }
    }
}
```

In the above code example, the `CurrentUICulture` is set based on the `CurrentLanguage` session variable. If a valid `CultureInfo` is not found, it will be defaulted to English. By default this session variable will not exist. A new action must be created in the Home Controller to allow the user to switch languages:

```
using System;
using System.Collections.Generic;
using System.Linq;
using System.Web;
```

```
using System.Web.Mvc;
using System.Globalization;

namespace MvcApplication4.Controllers
{
    public class HomeController : Controller
    {
        public ActionResult Index()
        {
            ViewBag.Message = "Welcome to ASP.NET MVC!";

            return View();
        }

        public ActionResult ChangeLanguage(string language)
        {
            Session["CurrentLanguage"] =
              new CultureInfo(language);
            return Redirect("Index");
        }

        public ActionResult About()
        {
            return View();
        }
    }
}
```

The new action ChangeLanguage accepts one parameter, the new language name. This is stored in the session variable that is referenced in the Global.asax.cs file. Finally, links must be created to switch languages. This should be available from every page, so the Shared _Layout.cshtml view must be edited to add the following links:

```
[ @Html.ActionLink("English", "ChangeLanguage", "Home",
    new { language = "en" }, null) ]
[ @Html.ActionLink("Français", "ChangeLanguage", "Home",
    new { language = "fr" }, null) ]
```

I've placed these beside the Log On link. As your website grows, it is now quite easy to add additional languages by creating a new resource file and adding a new link allowing the user to select the new language.

In the original problem I discussed the English dialect having multiple versions for Canada, USA, UK, etc. If you wish to separate a language by country, you can add a hyphen (-) and the country code after the language code. For example, en-GB would be used for English in the UK. You would also need to update your links to include this in the language name so that CurrentUICulture will be updated properly.

See Also

CurrentUICulture   (*http://msdn.microsoft.com/en-us/library/system.threading.thread .currentuiculture.aspx*)

1.5 Sending a Welcome Email

Problem

Many sites require people to register to access content or post a comment. With so many websites, it's quite difficult for people to remember each site they have registered for. By updating the registration process, an email can be sent that reminds the user where they just signed up, so they are able to return again later.

Solution

Implement the SmtpClient and MailMessage classes to send email to a user after registering.

Discussion

To send an email you need to configure an SMTP server, port, username, and password. To allow for easy configuration, I would suggest placing these in the appSettings of your Web.config file:

```
<appSettings>
  <add key="webpages:Version" value="1.0.0.0" />
  <add key="ClientValidationEnabled" value="true" />
  <add key="UnobtrusiveJavaScriptEnabled" value="true" />
  <add key="smtpServer" value="localhost" />
  <add key="smtpPort" value="25" />
  <add key="smtpUser" value="" />
  <add key="smtpPass" value="" />
  <add key="adminEmail" value="no-reply@no-reply.com" />
</appSettings>
```

These values should be updated as necessary to reflect your SMTP server, port, username, and password.

 If this is for a website that will require a development server as well as a live or staging environment, placing configuration settings in your Web.config provides the ability to use Visual Studio's XML transformations to easily update for the different environments.

To help organize the project a new folder and class will be created to contain the functions necessary to send emails. Right-click on the project and select *Add→New Folder* and name it Utils. Now right-click on the newly created Utils folder, select *Add→Class*, and name it MailClient.cs.

The MailClient class and its functions will be defined as static to provide easy access to the class and its functions. When it is integrated into future functions it won't require instantiating new objects. Below is a complete listing of the MailClient class:

```csharp
using System;
using System.Collections.Generic;
using System.Linq;
using System.Web;
using System.Net.Mail;
using System.Net;
using System.Configuration;

namespace MvcApplication4.Utils
{
    public static class MailClient
    {
        private static readonly SmtpClient Client;

        static MailClient()
        {
            Client = new SmtpClient
            {
                Host =
                  ConfigurationManager.AppSettings["SmtpServer"],
                Port =
                  Convert.ToInt32(
                    ConfigurationManager.AppSettings["SmtpPort"]),
                DeliveryMethod = SmtpDeliveryMethod.Network
            };
            Client.UseDefaultCredentials = false;
            Client.Credentials = new NetworkCredential(
                ConfigurationManager.AppSettings["SmtpUser"],
                ConfigurationManager.AppSettings["SmtpPass"]);
        }

        private static bool SendMessage(string from, string to,
            string subject, string body)
        {
            MailMessage mm = null;
            bool isSent = false;
            try
            {
                // Create our message
                mm = new MailMessage(from, to, subject, body);
                mm.DeliveryNotificationOptions =
                        DeliveryNotificationOptions.OnFailure;

                // Send it
                Client.Send(mm);
                isSent = true;
            }
            // Catch any errors, these should be logged and
            // dealt with later
            catch (Exception ex)
            {
                // If you wish to log email errors,
                // add it here...
                var exMsg = ex.Message;
            }
```

```
        finally
        {
            mm.Dispose();
        }

        return isSent;
    }

    public static bool SendWelcome(string email)
    {
        string body = "Put welcome email content here...";

        return SendMessage(
            ConfigurationManager.AppSettings["adminEmail"],
                email, "Welcome message", body);
    }
  }
}
```

The class begins by instantiating a new `SmtpClient` variable with the settings defined from the `Web.config`. Next a `SendMessage` function is created. This function is private and should not be called directly from outside of this class. This function is what performs the actual sending. It creates a new `MailMessage` object and sends it through the `SmtpClient` object created earlier. Finally, a `SendWelcome` function is created that accepts the users email address. It generates a generic message that should be updated to send your welcome email and it is sent by calling the `SendMessage` function.

To actually send the email after the user registers, the `Register` function in the `Account Controller` must be updated to call the `SendWelcome` function after the user is successfully created:

```
using System;
using System.Collections.Generic;
using System.Linq;
using System.Web;
using System.Web.Mvc;
using System.Web.Routing;
using System.Web.Security;
using MvcApplication4.Models;
using MvcApplication4.Utils;

namespace MvcApplication4.Controllers
{
    public class AccountController : Controller
    {
        ...

        //
        // POST: /Account/Register

        [HttpPost]
        public ActionResult Register(RegisterModel model)
        {
```

```
if (ModelState.IsValid)
{
    // Attempt to register the user
    MembershipCreateStatus createStatus;
    Membership.CreateUser(model.UserName,
        model.Password, model.Email, null, null,
        true, null, out createStatus);

    if (createStatus ==
            MembershipCreateStatus.Success)
    {
        // Send welcome email
        MailClient.SendWelcome(model.Email);
        FormsAuthentication.SetAuthCookie(
            model.UserName,
            false /* createPersistentCookie */);
        return RedirectToAction("Index", "Home");
    }
    else
    {
        ModelState.AddModelError("",
            ErrorCodeToString(createStatus));
    }
}

// If we got this far, something failed,
// redisplay form
return View(model);
        }
    }
}
```

The preceding code contains a basic example to extend your registration process to send a user a welcome email. In today's society, with the number of automated form processing applications that exist, it might be a good idea to further this example and change it from a welcome email to a "verify your email address" message. This could be done by updating the email to click a link in the welcome email that validates the account before the user can log in.

See Also

SmtpClient (*http://msdn.microsoft.com/en-us/library/system.net.mail.smtpclient.aspx*) and MailMessage (*http://msdn.microsoft.com/en-us/library/system.net.mail.mailmes sage.aspx*)

1.6 Retrieving a Forgotten Password

Problem

You or one of your website users have registered on your site and now they cannot remember their password and need a way to retrieve it.

Solution

To allow users to retrieve their password, a new action and view must be added to the `AccountController`. The function will use the `Membership` class to search for a matching user and send them an email containing their password.

Discussion

By default, MVC Internet Applications perform a one-way hash of the passwords making them impossible to retrieve. In the example below, the default encryption method will be changed to a two-way hash. It's not quite as secure, but it avoids forcing the user to reset their password if they forgot it.

To start, the `membership` settings in `Web.config` file needs to be adjusted:

```xml
<?xml version="1.0"?>
<configuration>
    ...

  <system.web>
    ...

    <membership>
      <providers>
        <clear />
        <add name="AspNetSqlMembershipProvider" type=
            "System.Web.Security.SqlMembershipProvider"
            connectionStringName="ApplicationServices"
            enablePasswordRetrieval="true" enablePasswordReset=
            "false" requiresQuestionAndAnswer="false"
            requiresUniqueEmail="false" passwordFormat=
            "Encrypted" maxInvalidPasswordAttempts="5"
            minRequiredPasswordLength="6"
            minRequiredNonalphanumericCharacters="0"
            passwordAttemptWindow="10" applicationName="/" />
      </providers>
    </membership>

    <machineKey
        validationKey=
"2CF9FF841A23366CFA5D655790D9308656B1F7532C0B95B5C067F80C45E59875
E2F3D68DAC63B5024C31D974D4BE151341FB8A31FC4BC3705DF5398B553FC3C3"
        decryptionKey="8E71407B62F47CCA3AAA6546B3880E1A0EF9833700
E0A0C511710F537E64B8B6" validation="SHA1" decryption="AES" />

    ...
  </system.web>

  ...
</configuration>
```

Four key items in the above example were changed/added:

1. enablePasswordRetrieval was changed from false to true
2. enablePasswordReset was changed from true to false
3. passwordFormat="Encrypted" was added
4. machineKey was generated for the encryption

With the configuration changes complete, a new model must be created for the Forgot Password view. This class should be placed in the AccountModels.cs class:

```
using System;
using System.Collections.Generic;
using System.ComponentModel.DataAnnotations;
using System.Globalization;
using System.Web.Mvc;
using System.Web.Security;

namespace MvcApplication4.Models
{

    public class ChangePasswordModel
    {
        ...
    }

    public class LogOnModel
    {
        ...
    }

    public class RegisterModel
    {
        ...
    }

    public class ForgotPasswordModel
    {
        [Required]
        [DataType(DataType.EmailAddress)]
        [Display(Name = "Email address")]
        public string Email { get; set; }
    }
}
```

Before the new view can be added, the application must be built. *Click Build→Build Solution* or press F6. Once the application has finished building, the new view can be added. Expand the Views folder and right-click on the Account folder and select *Add→View* (Figure 1-4). This view will be called ForgotPassword. Because this view will be strongly-typed to the ForgotPasswordModel previously created, be sure that it is selected from the Model class drop-down menu.

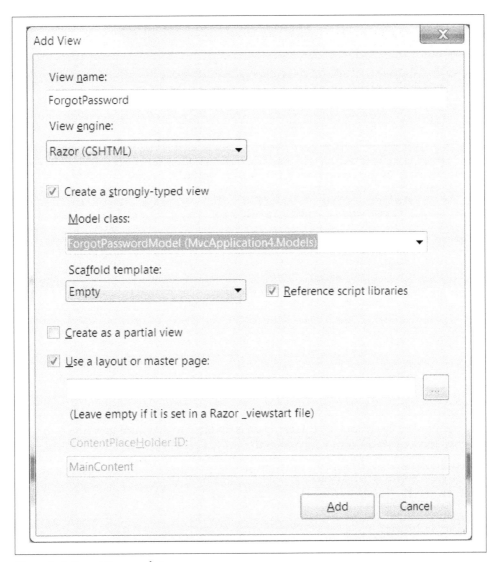

Figure 1-4. Forgot Password view

After the view is created, a form is added to it. The form is quite basic—it accepts the user's email address:

```
@model MvcApplication4.Models.ForgotPasswordModel

@{
    ViewBag.Title = "ForgotPassword";
}

<h2>ForgotPassword</h2>
```

```
<p>
    Use the form below to retrieve your password.
</p>

<script src="@Url.Content("~/Scripts/jquery.validate.min.js")"
    type="text/javascript"></script>
<script src="@Url.Content(
    "~/Scripts/jquery.validate.unobtrusive.min.js")"
    type="text/javascript"></script>

@using (Html.BeginForm()) {
    @Html.ValidationSummary(true, "Password retrieval was
unsuccessful. Please correct the errors and try again.")
    <div>
        <fieldset>
            <legend>Account Information</legend>

            <div class="editor-label">
                @Html.LabelFor(m => m.Email)
            </div>
            <div class="editor-field">
                @Html.TextBoxFor(m => m.Email)
                @Html.ValidationMessageFor(m => m.Email)
            </div>

            <p>
                <input type="submit" value="Retrieve Password" />
            </p>
        </fieldset>
    </div>
}
```

Next the previously created `MailClient` class is updated to include a new function that will send the user their forgotten password:

```
using System;
using System.Collections.Generic;
using System.Linq;
using System.Web;
using System.Net.Mail;
using System.Net;
using System.Configuration;

namespace MvcApplication4.Utils
{
    public class MailClient
    {
        private static readonly SmtpClient Client;

        static MailClient()
        {
            ...
        }

        private static bool SendMessage(string from, string to,
            string subject, string body)
```

```
        {
            ...
        }

        public static bool SendWelcome(string email)
        {
            ...
        }

        public static bool SendLostPassword(string email,
            string password)
        {
            string body = "Your password is: " + password;

            return SendMessage("no-reply@no-reply.com", email,
                "Lost Password", body);
        }
    }
}
```

This function is very similar to the previous one, with the exception that a second parameter is added—the user's password. The password is added to the body of the email being sent to the user.

Finally, inside of the AccountController, two ForgotPassword functions are created. The first function will simply load the previously created view. The second function will accept the ForgotPasswordModel form that is posted. Using the email address collected in the form, it will search the Membership database for users matching that email address. For each user that is found, one email will be sent to them with their password:

```
using System;
using System.Collections.Generic;
using System.Linq;
using System.Web;
using System.Web.Mvc;
using System.Web.Routing;
using System.Web.Security;
using MvcApplication4.Models;
using MvcApplication4.Utils;

namespace MvcApplication4.Controllers
{
    public class AccountController : Controller
    {
        ...

        //
        // Get: /Account/ForgotPassword

        public ActionResult ForgotPassword()
        {
            return View();
        }
```

```
//
// Post: /Account/ForgotPassword
[HttpPost]
public ActionResult ForgotPassword(
    ForgotPasswordModel model)
{
    if (ModelState.IsValid)
    {
        MembershipUserCollection users =
            Membership.FindUsersByEmail(model.Email);
        if (users.Count > 0)
        {
            foreach (MembershipUser user in users)
            {
                MailClient.SendLostPassword(model.Email,
                  user.GetPassword());
            }

            return RedirectToAction("LogOn");
        }
    }

    // If we got this far, something failed,
    // redisplay form
    return View(model);
}

...

    }
}
```

In the last two recipes, basic emails have been sent to the users. These examples can easily be enhanced to send more complex emails or even emails containing HTML content. To send HTML emails, there is a boolean variable IsBodyHtml on the Mail Message class that can be set to true.

See Also

Membership.Providers Property (*http://msdn.microsoft.com/en-us/library/system.web .security.membership.providers.aspx*)

1.7 Sorting a List of Results

Problem

You have a large list (say, a list of books), and you cannot easily find the one you are looking for. Sorting them by one of the columns in the list should help you find what you are looking for faster.

Solution

Update the list of books to make the column headings a link. Once the link is clicked on, implement the *Dynamic Linq Library* to sort the results based on the column selected (ascending or descending—clicking the link again will reverse the order).

Discussion

I was a bit surprised by the effort required to add sorting to the automatically generated views, compared to other frameworks I've used. Hopefully in future versions of MVC, this will become a part of the scaffolding process. The other part that I thought required quite a bit of effort was the example provided on the homepage of ASP.NET MVC where you need to use a switch statement with one case per sorting option. In the case of the book example, there are only five columns to be sorted, so it wouldn't be too bad—but as this functionality gets replicated to other lists, perhaps authors, etc., the work will continue to grow. In the example below, the work is simplified by taking advantage of the *Dynamic Linq Library*.

By default, the Linq library being used allows for strongly-typed expressions to build results from a database. This provides some great advantages, such as full IntelliSense support and compiler-time error messages if a mistake is made. However, as I mentioned above, it also becomes a lot of work to build useful functionality.

To add sorting both the BooksController and the Books/Index view require changes. Below is the updated index view:

```
@model IEnumerable<MvcApplication4.Models.Book>

<h2>@ViewBag.Title</h2>

<p>
    @Html.ActionLink((string)ViewBag.CreateLink, "Create")
</p>
<table>
    <tr>
        <th>
            @Html.ActionLink((string)ViewBag.TitleDisplay,
              "Index", new { sortOrder = ViewBag.TitleSortParam })
        </th>
        <th>
            @Html.ActionLink((string)ViewBag.IsbnDisplay,
              "Index", new { sortOrder = ViewBag.IsbnSortParam })
        </th>
        <th>
            @ViewBag.SummaryDisplay
        </th>
        <th>
            @Html.ActionLink((string)ViewBag.AuthorDisplay,
              "Index", new { sortOrder = ViewBag.AuthorSortParam })
        </th>
```

```
                <th>
                    @ViewBag.ThumbnailDisplay
                </th>
                <th>
                    @Html.ActionLink((string)ViewBag.PriceDisplay,
                      "Index", new { sortOrder = ViewBag.PriceSortParam })
                </th>
                <th>
                    @Html.ActionLink((string)ViewBag.PublishedDisplay,
                      "Index", new { sortOrder =
                        ViewBag.PublishedSortParam })
                </th>
                <th></th>
            </tr>

    @foreach (var item in Model) {
            <tr>
                <td>
                    @Html.DisplayFor(modelItem => item.Title)
                </td>
                <td>
                    @Html.DisplayFor(modelItem => item.Isbn)
                </td>
                <td>
                    @Html.DisplayFor(modelItem => item.Summary)
                </td>
                <td>
                    @Html.DisplayFor(modelItem => item.Author)
                </td>
                <td>
                    @Html.DisplayFor(modelItem => item.Thumbnail)
                </td>
                <td>
                    @Html.DisplayFor(modelItem => item.Price)
                </td>
                <td>
                    @Html.DisplayFor(modelItem => item.Published)
                </td>
                <td>
                    @Html.ActionLink((string)ViewBag.EditLink,
                      "Edit", new { id=item.ID }) |
                    @Html.ActionLink((string)ViewBag.DetailsLink,
                      "Details", new { id = item.ID }) |
                    @Html.ActionLink((string)ViewBag.DeleteLink,
                      "Delete", new { id = item.ID })
                </td>
            </tr>
    }

    </table>
```

In the above example, the previously created <th> tags have been updated to no longer be static text, instead they have been converted to HTML links using the ActionLink function from the HTML helper.

Next the `BookController`'s `Index()` function needs to be updated. This function will accept a new parameter called `sortOrder`. This variable will then be used to perform a *Dynamic Linq* query to sort the results by this column. A few new `ViewBag` variables are also created that contains the sort condition used by each column.

Microsoft has provided a free `DynamicQuery` class that extends the `Linq` namespace, allowing you to build dynamic queries by building expressions. To download the library for C#, visit *http://msdn2.microsoft.com/en-us/vcsharp/bb894665.aspx*. Once downloaded, you will need to extract the files to a location on your hard drive. The dynamic LINQ library class can be found here: `~\CSharpSamples\LinqSamples\Dynamic Query\DynamicQuery\Dynamic.cs`. This file must be added to the project. For organization purposes I would suggest adding it to the previously created `Utils` directory. Right-click on the `Utils` directory and select *Add→Existing Item* and navigate to the dynamic class (or you can drag the file from the folder onto the `Utils` folder in your MVC application).

Once added the `BooksController` is updated as follows:

```
using System;
using System.Collections.Generic;
using System.Data;
using System.Data.Entity;
using System.Linq;
using System.Linq.Dynamic;
using System.Web;
using System.Web.Mvc;
using MvcApplication4.Models;
using MvcApplication4.Resources;

namespace MvcApplication4.Controllers
{
    public class BooksController : Controller
    {
        private BookDBContext db = new BookDBContext();

        //
        // GET: /Books/

        public ViewResult Index(string sortOrder)
        {
            #region ViewBag Resources
            ...
            #endregion

            #region ViewBag Sort Params
            // Define the sort orders - if the same link is
            // clicked twice, reverse the direction from
            // ascending to descending
            ViewBag.TitleSortParam = (sortOrder == "Title")
                ? "Title desc" : "Title";
            ViewBag.IsbnSortParam = (sortOrder == "Isbn")
                ? "Isbn desc" : "Isbn";
```

```
ViewBag.AuthorSortParam = (sortOrder == "Author")
    ? "Author desc" : "Author";
ViewBag.PriceSortParam = (sortOrder == "Price")
    ? "Price desc" : "Price";
ViewBag.PublishedSortParam =
    (String.IsNullOrEmpty(sortOrder))
        ? "Published desc" : "";

// Default the sort order
if (String.IsNullOrEmpty(sortOrder))
{
    sortOrder = "Published desc";
}
#endregion

var books = db.Books.OrderBy(sortOrder);

return View(books.ToList());
}

    ...
    }
}
```

 The above example allows sorting based on the sortOrder variable passed in. The code above is slightly insecure and is meant to demonstrate the process of performing dynamic LINQ queries with minimal effort. Because this variable can be passed in through the URL, it is important to add some more validation around the inputted data to ensure a user is not attempting something malicious.

See Also

System.Linq.Expressions Namespace (*http://msdn.microsoft.com/en-us/library/system .linq.expressions.aspx*)

1.8 Paging Through a List of Results

Problem

You have a long list of results that either take too long to load, or you simply can't find the result you are looking for in the long list. Breaking the results up into multiple pages will reduce the page load time and help find results faster, especially when the results are sorted.

Solution

Implement PagedList.MVC to navigate between pages of a list of records.

Discussion

To add paging to an application you need to install a new library called `Paged List.Mvc` through the *NuGet Library*. This will allow a paged list of books rather than the complete list. To install the package, select the *Tools menu→Library Package Manager→Add Library Package Reference*. From the left, select the Online button. In the search box, enter `PagedList` and click the *Install* button beside the `PagedList.MVC` package (see Figure 1-5).

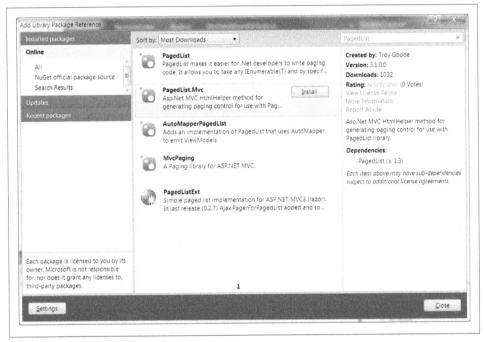

Figure 1-5. PagedList.MVC library package

Once the `PagedList` is installed, the code to create the pagination links will be added as a partial view. This will allow the code to be reused on future lists that require paging of results. Because the paging process doesn't really contain many dynamic variables, this is a perfect opportunity to reuse the HTML on every list of results with very minimal effort, while maintaining a consistent look.

 A partial view is a great spot to place reusable HTML code that doesn't belong to any one view—or as in the example below—that will be used multiple times.

To begin, expand the Views folder and right-click on the Shared folder and select *Add→View*. In the dialog box, enter the name as _Paging and be sure to select the checkbox for *Create as partial view*. When you are done, press *Add*. The content for the new view is as follows:

```
<p>
    @if (Model.HasPreviousPage)
    {
        @Html.ActionLink("<< First", "Index", new {
          page = 1, sortOrder = ViewBag.CurrentSortOrder })
        @Html.Raw(" ");
        @Html.ActionLink("< Prev", "Index", new {
          page = Model.PageNumber - 1, sortOrder =
              ViewBag.CurrentSortOrder })
    }
    else
    {
        @:<< First
        @Html.Raw(" ");
        @:< Prev
    }

      

    @if (Model.HasNextPage)
    {
        @Html.ActionLink("Next >", "Index", new {
          page = Model.PageNumber + 1,
              sortOrder = ViewBag.CurrentSortOrder })
        @Html.Raw(" ");
        @Html.ActionLink("Last >>", "Index", new {
          page = Model.PageCount,
              sortOrder = ViewBag.CurrentSortOrder })
    }
    else
    {
        @:Next >
        @Html.Raw(" ")
        @:Last >>
    }
</p>
```

The following partial view creates up to four links: first, previous, next, and last. I say up to four because if there are no previous pages available, the first and previous link are disabled. Same for when there is no next page: the next and last links are disabled. Each link passes two variables to the Index() function: a page number and the current sort order. The current sort order is passed to ensure that when switching between pages, the user doesn't lose the sorting they chose.

Next, the Books/Index view needs a few changes:

```
@model PagedList.IPagedList<MvcApplication4.Models.Book>

<h2>@ViewBag.Title</h2>
```

```
<p>
    @Html.ActionLink((string)ViewBag.CreateLink, "Create")
</p>

@Html.Partial("_Paging")

<table>
    <tr>
        <th>
            @Html.ActionLink((string)ViewBag.TitleDisplay,
              "Index", new { sortOrder = ViewBag.TitleSortParam })
        </th>
        <th>
            @Html.ActionLink((string)ViewBag.IsbnDisplay,
              "Index", new { sortOrder = ViewBag.IsbnSortParam })
        </th>
        <th>
            @ViewBag.SummaryDisplay
        </th>
        <th>
            @Html.ActionLink((string)ViewBag.AuthorDisplay,
              "Index", new { sortOrder =
                ViewBag.AuthorSortParam })
        </th>
        <th>
            @ViewBag.ThumbnailDisplay
        </th>
        <th>
            @Html.ActionLink((string)ViewBag.PriceDisplay,
              "Index", new { sortOrder = ViewBag.PriceSortParam })
        </th>
        <th>
            @Html.ActionLink((string)ViewBag.PublishedDisplay,
              "Index", new { sortOrder =
                ViewBag.PublishedSortParam })
        </th>
        <th></th>
    </tr>

@foreach (var item in Model) {
    <tr>
        <td>
            @Html.DisplayFor(modelItem => item.Title)
        </td>
        <td>
            @Html.DisplayFor(modelItem => item.Isbn)
        </td>
        <td>
            @Html.DisplayFor(modelItem => item.Summary)
        </td>
        <td>
            @Html.DisplayFor(modelItem => item.Author)
        </td>
```

```
<td>
    @Html.DisplayFor(modelItem => item.Thumbnail)
</td>
<td>
    @Html.DisplayFor(modelItem => item.Price)
</td>
<td>
    @Html.DisplayFor(modelItem => item.Published)
</td>
<td>
    @Html.ActionLink((string)ViewBag.EditLink,
        "Edit", new { id=item.ID }) |
    @Html.ActionLink((string)ViewBag.DetailsLink,
        "Details", new { id = item.ID }) |
    @Html.ActionLink((string)ViewBag.DeleteLink,
        "Delete", new { id = item.ID })
</td>
    </tr>
}

</table>

@Html.Partial("_Paging")
```

The above example contains three subtle changes to the view. Firstly, the strongly-typed model has been updated to be of type `PagedList.IPagedList` and the shared `_Paging` view has been included twice: once above the table and once below the table.

 You might notice that the sorting links were not updated to include the page number like the paging links were. This is done purposely, as the expected functionality of changing the sort order is to begin back at page 1 again.

Finally, the `BooksController` needs to be updated as well. The `Index()` function is updated to accept a new parameter, page, and instead of returning the books as a list, the books are being returned as a paged list instead. Also, inside of the sort order region, a new `ViewBag` variable has been added that sets the current sort order (used in the `_Paging` partial view):

```
using System;
using System.Collections.Generic;
using System.Data;
using System.Data.Entity;
using System.Linq;
using System.Linq.Dynamic;
using System.Web;
using System.Web.Mvc;
using MvcApplication4.Models;
using MvcApplication4.Utils;
using PagedList;
```

```
namespace MvcApplication4.Controllers
{
    public class BooksController : Controller
    {
        private BookDBContext db = new BookDBContext();

        //
        // GET: /Books/

        public ViewResult Index(string sortOrder, int page = 1)
        {
            #region ViewBag Resources
            ...
            #endregion

            #region ViewBag Sort Params
            ...
            ViewBag.CurrentSortOrder = sortOrder;
            #endregion

            var books = db.Books.OrderBy(sortOrder);

            int maxRecords = 1;
            int currentPage = page - 1;
            return View(books.ToPagedList(currentPage,
                maxRecords));
        }

        ...
    }
}
```

If you wish to further extend the partial view to reuse in other list results, you only need to ensure that the same `ViewBag` variables are set for each list. In case the list results aren't in the Index action like this one is, you could update the `Html.ActionLink` calls to potentially use another `ViewBag` variable that defines the action—making it dynamic.

1.9 Filtering a List of Results

Problem

When sorting and paging are not enough to help users find their results, filtering by specific content is another way to help users find what they are looking for.

Solution

Add new links to allow a user to filter a list of results by predefined criteria and using the `Linq` library to perform the filtering of data.

Discussion

To add filter links, changes need to be made to both the `Books/Index` view and the `BooksController`. The changes to the view are quite similar to the previous two recipes. HTML links must be added that allow the user to choose how they want to filter the content. Three new links will be added: All, New Releases, and Coming Soon. New Releases will be defined as something published within the last 2 weeks, and Coming Soon is defined as something not yet published.

Below is the new `Books/Index` view. The three new links all contain the current sort order as a parameter (to maintain the user's current sort option) and the last two links contain a new variable called filter. Like the paging links, if the active filter is the link that should be displayed, it is not set as a link and text is displayed to identify to the user the current filter option. To ensure the filter is maintained when the user changes the sort order, those links are also updated to pass the current filter as well:

```
@model PagedList.IPagedList<MvcApplication4.Models.Book>

<h2>@MvcApplication4.Resources.Resource1.BookIndexTitle</h2>

<p>
    @Html.ActionLink("Create New", "Create")
</p>
<p>
    Show:
    @if (ViewBag.CurrentFilter != "")
    {
        @Html.ActionLink("All", "Index", new {
                sortOrder = ViewBag.CurrentSortOrder })
    }
    else
    {
        @:All
    }
      |  
    @if (ViewBag.CurrentFilter != "NewReleases")
    {
        @Html.ActionLink("New Releases", "Index", new {
                filter = "NewReleases", sortOrder =
                    ViewBag.CurrentSortOrder })
    }
    else
    {
        @:New Releases
    }
      |  
    @if (ViewBag.CurrentFilter != "ComingSoon")
    {
        @Html.ActionLink("Coming Soon", "Index", new {
                filter = "ComingSoon", sortOrder =
                    ViewBag.CurrentSortOrder })
    }
```

```
        else
        {
            @:Coming Soon
        }
    </p>
    @Html.Partial("_Paging")
    <table>
        <tr>
            <th>
                @Html.ActionLink("Title", "Index", new {
                    sortOrder = ViewBag.TitleSortParam,
                    filter = ViewBag.CurrentFilter })
            </th>
            <th>
                @Html.ActionLink("Isbn", "Index", new {
                    sortOrder = ViewBag.IsbnSortParam,
                    filter = ViewBag.CurrentFilter })
            </th>
            <th>
                Summary
            </th>
            <th>
                @Html.ActionLink("Author", "Index", new {
                    sortOrder = ViewBag.AuthorSortParam,
                    filter = ViewBag.CurrentFilter })
            </th>
            <th>
                Thumbnail
            </th>
            <th>
                @Html.ActionLink("Price", "Index", new {
                    sortOrder = ViewBag.PriceSortParam,
                    filter = ViewBag.CurrentFilter })
            </th>
            <th>
                @Html.ActionLink("Published", "Index", new {
                    sortOrder = ViewBag.PublishedSortParam,
                    filter = ViewBag.CurrentFilter })
            </th>
            <th></th>
        </tr>

    @foreach (var item in Model)
    {
        <tr>
            <td>
                @Html.DisplayFor(modelItem => item.Title)
            </td>
            <td>
                @Html.DisplayFor(modelItem => item.Isbn)
            </td>
            <td>
                @Html.DisplayFor(modelItem => item.Summary)
            </td>
```

```
        <td>
            @Html.DisplayFor(modelItem => item.Author)
        </td>
        <td>
            @Html.DisplayFor(modelItem => item.Thumbnail)
        </td>
        <td>
            @Html.DisplayFor(modelItem => item.Price)
        </td>
        <td>
            @Html.DisplayFor(modelItem => item.Published)
        </td>
        <td>
            @Html.ActionLink("Edit",
                "Edit", new { id = item.ID }) |
            @Html.ActionLink("Details",
                "Details", new { id = item.ID }) |
            @Html.ActionLink("Delete",
                "Delete", new { id = item.ID })
        </td>
    </tr>
}

</table>

@Html.Partial("_Paging")
```

The partial view for the paging links created in the last recipe also requires updating. In the example below, the four paging links have been updated to pass the current filter option along with the page and sort order values:

```
<p>
    @if (Model.HasPreviousPage)
    {
        @Html.ActionLink("<< First", "Index", new {
                page = 1,
                sortOrder = ViewBag.CurrentSortOrder,
                filter = ViewBag.CurrentFilter })
        @Html.Raw(" ");
        @Html.ActionLink("< Prev", "Index", new {
                page = Model.PageNumber - 1,
                sortOrder = ViewBag.CurrentSortOrder,
                filter = ViewBag.CurrentFilter })
    }
    else
    {
        @:<< First
        @Html.Raw(" ");
        @:< Prev
    }

      

    @if (Model.HasNextPage)
    {
```

```
            @Html.ActionLink("Next >", "Index", new {
                    page = Model.PageNumber + 1,
                    sortOrder = ViewBag.CurrentSortOrder,
                    filter = ViewBag.CurrentFilter })
            @Html.Raw(" ");
            @Html.ActionLink("Last >>", "Index", new {
                    page = Model.PageCount,
                    sortOrder = ViewBag.CurrentSortOrder,
                    filter = ViewBag.CurrentFilter })
        }
        else
        {
            @:Next >
            @Html.Raw(" ")
            @:Last >>
        }
    </p>
```

Next are the changes to the BooksController. The Index() function is being updated again. It is now accepting a new variable for the filter. Based on the filter options, the list of books will be reduced based on the user's selection. There are two approaches that could be used to implement the filtering:

1. Use dynamic Linq again to create a string-based where clause

2. Use standard Linq and a switch statement to create a strongly-typed where clause

Because filter links typically don't contain too many entries compared to sortable headers, this recipe will use the second approach. By using the second approach, the warning in the sorting recipe doesn't need to be considered because it is strongly-typed and not dynamic, so extra checking of the input is not required to prevent dangerous SQL injection.

```
using System;
using System.Collections.Generic;
using System.Data;
using System.Data.Entity;
using System.Linq;
using System.Linq.Dynamic;
using System.Web;
using System.Web.Mvc;
using MvcApplication4.Models;
using MvcApplication4.Utils;
using PagedList;

namespace MvcApplication4.Controllers
{
    public class BooksController : Controller
    {
        private BookDBContext db = new BookDBContext();

        //
        // GET: /Books/
```

```
public ViewResult Index(string sortOrder,
    string filter, int page = 1)
{
    #region ViewBag Resources
    ...
    #endregion

    #region ViewBag Sort Params
    ...
    #endregion

    var books = from b in db.Books select b;

    #region Filter Switch
    switch (filter)
    {
        case "NewReleases":
            var startDate = DateTime.Today.AddDays(-14);
            books = books.Where(b => b.Published
                <= DateTime.Today.Date
                && b.Published >= startDate
            );
            break;

        case "ComingSoon":
            books = books.Where(b => b.Published >
                DateTime.Today.Date);
            break;

        default:
            // No filter needed
            break;
    }

    ViewBag.CurrentFilter =
        String.IsNullOrEmpty(filter) ? "" : filter;
    #endregion

    books = books.OrderBy(sortOrder);

    int maxRecords = 1;
    int currentPage = page - 1;
    return View(books.ToPagedList(currentPage,
        maxRecords));
}

...
}
}
```

In the above example, if the user chose to filter by New Releases, a search is performed to return any books that were published today or within the past 14 days. Or if the user chose Coming Soon, a search is performed to return any books that will be published after today. Otherwise, no filtering is required and all books are returned.

1.10 Searching a List of Results by Keyword

Problem

When sorting, paging, and filtering are not enough to help you find what you are look-ing for, the next best alternative is to let the user type what they want to find.

Solution

Create a new form and text input with the Html Helper and update the previous filtered results by the user-entered keyword with the Linq library.

Discussion

Much like the previous recipes, adding a keyword search requires changes to both the Books/Index view and BooksController. The view will be changed by adding a new form and textbox input for the user to enter their keyword of choice. Also, to ensure that the user's keyword is maintained when changing the sort order, filter, or paging through links, the code will be updated to maintain the user's keyword. The example below contains the updated Books/Index view:

```
@model PagedList.IPagedList<MvcApplication4.Models.Book>

<h2>@MvcApplication4.Resources.Resource1.BookIndexTitle</h2>

<p>
    @Html.ActionLink("Create New", "Create")
</p>
<p>
    Show:
    @if (ViewBag.CurrentFilter != "")
    {
        @Html.ActionLink("All", "Index", new {
                sortOrder = ViewBag.CurrentSortOrder,
                Keyword = ViewBag.CurrentKeyword })
    }
    else
    {
        @:All
    }
      |  
    @if (ViewBag.CurrentFilter != "NewReleases")
    {
        @Html.ActionLink("New Releases", "Index", new {
                filter = "NewReleases",
                sortOrder = ViewBag.CurrentSortOrder,
                Keyword = ViewBag.CurrentKeyword })
    }
    else
    {
        @:New Releases
    }
```

```
      |  
    @if (ViewBag.CurrentFilter != "ComingSoon")
    {
        @Html.ActionLink("Coming Soon", "Index", new {
                filter = "ComingSoon",
                sortOrder = ViewBag.CurrentSortOrder,
                Keyword = ViewBag.CurrentKeyword })
    }
    else
    {
        @:Coming Soon
    }
</p>
@using (Html.BeginForm())
{
    @:Search: @Html.TextBox("Keyword")
    <input type="submit" value="Search" />
}
@Html.Partial("_Paging")
<table>
    <tr>
        <th>
            @Html.ActionLink("Title", "Index", new {
                sortOrder = ViewBag.TitleSortParam,
                filter = ViewBag.CurrentFilter,
                Keyword = ViewBag.CurrentKeyword })
        </th>
        <th>
            @Html.ActionLink("Isbn", "Index", new {
                sortOrder = ViewBag.IsbnSortParam,
                filter = ViewBag.CurrentFilter,
                Keyword = ViewBag.CurrentKeyword })
        </th>
        <th>
            Summary
        </th>
        <th>
            @Html.ActionLink("Author", "Index", new {
                sortOrder = ViewBag.AuthorSortParam,
                filter = ViewBag.CurrentFilter,
                Keyword = ViewBag.CurrentKeyword })
        </th>
        <th>
            Thumbnail
        </th>
        <th>
            @Html.ActionLink("Price", "Index", new {
                sortOrder = ViewBag.PriceSortParam,

                filter = ViewBag.CurrentFilter,
                Keyword = ViewBag.CurrentKeyword })
        </th>
        <th>
            @Html.ActionLink("Published", "Index", new {
                sortOrder = ViewBag.PublishedSortParam,
```

```
                    filter = ViewBag.CurrentFilter,
                    Keyword = ViewBag.CurrentKeyword })
            </th>
            <th></th>
        </tr>

    @foreach (var item in Model)
    {
        <tr>
            <td>
                @Html.DisplayFor(modelItem => item.Title)
            </td>
            <td>
                @Html.DisplayFor(modelItem => item.Isbn)
            </td>
            <td>
                @Html.DisplayFor(modelItem => item.Summary)
            </td>
            <td>
                @Html.DisplayFor(modelItem => item.Author)
            </td>
            <td>
                @Html.DisplayFor(modelItem => item.Thumbnail)
            </td>
            <td>
                @Html.DisplayFor(modelItem => item.Price)
            </td>
            <td>
                @Html.DisplayFor(modelItem => item.Published)
            </td>
            <td>
                @Html.ActionLink("Edit",
                    "Edit", new { id = item.ID }) |
                @Html.ActionLink("Details",
                    "Details", new { id = item.ID }) |
                @Html.ActionLink("Delete",
                    "Delete", new { id = item.ID })
            </td>
        </tr>
    }

    </table>

    @Html.Partial("_Paging")
```

The shared paging view also needs to be updated to maintain the current keyword as well:

```
<p>
    @if (Model.HasPreviousPage)
    {
        @Html.ActionLink("<< First", "Index", new {
                page = 1,
                sortOrder = ViewBag.CurrentSortOrder,
                filter = ViewBag.CurrentFilter,
                Keyword = ViewBag.CurrentKeyword })
```

```
            @Html.Raw(" ");
            @Html.ActionLink("< Prev", "Index", new {
                    page = Model.PageNumber - 1,
                    sortOrder = ViewBag.CurrentSortOrder,
                    filter = ViewBag.CurrentFilter,
                    Keyword = ViewBag.CurrentKeyword })
        }
        else
        {
            @:<< First
            @Html.Raw(" ");
            @:< Prev
        }

          

        @if (Model.HasNextPage)
        {
            @Html.ActionLink("Next >", "Index", new {
                    page = Model.PageNumber + 1,
                    sortOrder = ViewBag.CurrentSortOrder,
                    filter = ViewBag.CurrentFilter,
                    Keyword = ViewBag.CurrentKeyword })
            @Html.Raw(" ");
            @Html.ActionLink("Last >>", "Index", new {
                    page = Model.PageCount,
                    sortOrder = ViewBag.CurrentSortOrder,
                    filter = ViewBag.CurrentFilter,
                    Keyword = ViewBag.CurrentKeyword })
        }
        else
        {
            @:Next >
            @Html.Raw(" ")
            @:Last >>
        }
    </p>
```

Finally the `BooksController` needs to be updated. In the example below, the `Index` function is updated to accept a new keyword parameter and if the user has entered a keyword the books title and author are searched by that keyword. If you wish to add other fields as well, simply update the example below to include the additional fields:

```
using System;
using System.Collections.Generic;
using System.Data;
using System.Data.Entity;
using System.Linq;
using System.Linq.Dynamic;
using System.Web;
using System.Web.Mvc;
using MvcApplication4.Models;
using MvcApplication4.Utils;
using PagedList;
```

```
namespace MvcApplication4.Controllers
{
    public class BooksController : Controller
    {
        private BookDBContext db = new BookDBContext();

        //
        // GET: /Books/

        public ViewResult Index(string sortOrder, string filter,
            string Keyword, int page = 1)
        {
            #region ViewBag Resources
            ...
            #endregion

            #region ViewBag Sort Params
            ...
            #endregion

            var books = from b in db.Books select b;

            #region Keyword Search
            if (!String.IsNullOrEmpty(Keyword))
            {
                books = books.Where(b =>
                    b.Title.ToUpper().Contains(Keyword.ToUpper())
                    || b.Author.ToUpper().Contains(
                        Keyword.ToUpper()));
            }
            ViewBag.CurrentKeyword =
                String.IsNullOrEmpty(Keyword) ? "" : Keyword;
            #endregion

            #region Filter Switch
            ...
            #endregion

            int maxRecords = 1;
            int currentPage = page - 1;
            return View(books.ToPagedList(currentPage,
                maxRecords));
        }

        ...

    }
}
```

1.11 Uploading a File Through a Form

Problem

You want to allow users to upload and save a file to your website.

Solution

Implement a file upload and save the file to disk using `HttpPostedFileBase`.

Discussion

In the following example, the previously created views to add and edit books will be updated to allow a user to select a file to upload for the thumbnail field. To begin the **Books/Create** view must be updated to change the `enctype` of the form and replace the scaffolded textbox for the thumbnail field. Below is the updated create view:

```
@model MvcApplication4.Models.Book

@{
    ViewBag.Title = "Create";
}

<h2>Create</h2>

<script src="@Url.Content("~/Scripts/jquery.validate.min.js")"
    type="text/javascript"></script>
<script src="
    @Url.Content("~/Scripts/jquery.validate.unobtrusive.min.js")"
    type="text/javascript"></script>

@using (Html.BeginForm("Create", "Books", FormMethod.Post,
        new { enctype = "multipart/form-data" }))
{
    @Html.ValidationSummary(true)
    <fieldset>
        <legend>Book</legend>

        <div class="editor-label">
            @Html.LabelFor(model => model.Title)
        </div>
        <div class="editor-field">
            @Html.EditorFor(model => model.Title)
            @Html.ValidationMessageFor(model => model.Title)
        </div>

        <div class="editor-label">
            @Html.LabelFor(model => model.Isbn)
        </div>
        <div class="editor-field">
            @Html.EditorFor(model => model.Isbn)
            @Html.ValidationMessageFor(model => model.Isbn)
        </div>
```

```
            <div class="editor-label">
                @Html.LabelFor(model => model.Summary)
            </div>
            <div class="editor-field">
                @Html.EditorFor(model => model.Summary)
                @Html.ValidationMessageFor(model => model.Summary)
            </div>

            <div class="editor-label">
                @Html.LabelFor(model => model.Author)
            </div>
            <div class="editor-field">
                @Html.EditorFor(model => model.Author)
                @Html.ValidationMessageFor(model => model.Author)
            </div>

            <div class="editor-label">
                @Html.LabelFor(model => model.Thumbnail)
            </div>
            <div class="editor-field">
                <input type="file" name="file" />
                @Html.ValidationMessageFor(model => model.Thumbnail)
            </div>

            <div class="editor-label">
                @Html.LabelFor(model => model.Price)
            </div>
            <div class="editor-field">
                @Html.EditorFor(model => model.Price)
                @Html.ValidationMessageFor(model => model.Price)
            </div>

            <div class="editor-label">
                @Html.LabelFor(model => model.Published)
            </div>
            <div class="editor-field">
                @Html.EditorFor(model => model.Published)
                @Html.ValidationMessageFor(model => model.Published)
            </div>

            <p>
                <input type="submit" value="Create" />
            </p>
        </fieldset>
    }

    <div>
        @Html.ActionLink("Back to List", "Index")
    </div>
```

The books edit view must also be updated in the same way, with the exception that a hidden field has been added (passing in the old thumbnail). This will be used in the BooksController to delete the old file before uploading the new file:

```
@model MvcApplication4.Models.Book

@{
    ViewBag.Title = "Edit";
}

<h2>Edit</h2>

<script src="@Url.Content("~/Scripts/jquery.validate.min.js")"
    type="text/javascript"></script>
<script src="
    @Url.Content("~/Scripts/jquery.validate.unobtrusive.min.js")"
    type="text/javascript"></script>

@using (Html.BeginForm("Edit", "Books", FormMethod.Post,
        new { enctype = "multipart/form-data" }))
{
    @Html.ValidationSummary(true)
    <fieldset>
        <legend>Book</legend>

        @Html.HiddenFor(model => model.ID)

        <div class="editor-label">
            @Html.LabelFor(model => model.Title)
        </div>
        <div class="editor-field">
            @Html.EditorFor(model => model.Title)
            @Html.ValidationMessageFor(model => model.Title)
        </div>

        <div class="editor-label">
            @Html.LabelFor(model => model.Isbn)
        </div>
        <div class="editor-field">
            @Html.EditorFor(model => model.Isbn)
            @Html.ValidationMessageFor(model => model.Isbn)
        </div>

        <div class="editor-label">
            @Html.LabelFor(model => model.Summary)
        </div>
        <div class="editor-field">
            @Html.EditorFor(model => model.Summary)
            @Html.ValidationMessageFor(model => model.Summary)
        </div>

        <div class="editor-label">
            @Html.LabelFor(model => model.Author)
        </div>
        <div class="editor-field">
            @Html.EditorFor(model => model.Author)
            @Html.ValidationMessageFor(model => model.Author)
        </div>
```

```
        <div class="editor-label">
            @Html.LabelFor(model => model.Thumbnail)
        </div>
        <div class="editor-field">
            <input type="file" name="file" />
            @Html.HiddenFor(model => model.Thumbnail)
            @Html.ValidationMessageFor(model => model.Thumbnail)
        </div>

        <div class="editor-label">
            @Html.LabelFor(model => model.Price)
        </div>
        <div class="editor-field">
            @Html.EditorFor(model => model.Price)
            @Html.ValidationMessageFor(model => model.Price)
        </div>

        <div class="editor-label">
            @Html.LabelFor(model => model.Published)
        </div>
        <div class="editor-field">
            @Html.EditorFor(model => model.Published)
            @Html.ValidationMessageFor(model => model.Published)
        </div>

        <p>
            <input type="submit" value="Save" />
        </p>
    </fieldset>
}

<div>
    @Html.ActionLink("Back to List", "Index")
</div>
```

Since both the Create and Edit functions in the BooksController will save the uploaded file, a new class will be created to avoid duplicating code. This class will be created in the Utils folder. With the Utils folder selected, right-click and select *Add→Class*. This class will be called FileUpload.cs.

This new class will be responsible for two key functions: saving the file and deleting the file. In the following example, the FileUpload class receives an HttpPostedFile Base variable and saves it to a specific spot on the web server. Another function does the opposite, it receives the name of the file and deletes it from the web server:

```
using System;
using System.Collections.Generic;
using System.Linq;
using System.Web;
using System.IO;

namespace MvcApplication4.Utils
{
    public static class FileUpload
```

```
{
    public static char DirSeparator =
        System.IO.Path.DirectorySeparatorChar;
    public static string FilesPath = "Content" +
        DirSeparator + "Uploads" + DirSeparator;

    public static string UploadFile(HttpPostedFileBase file)
    {
        // Check if we have a file
        if (null == file) return "";
        // Make sure the file has content
        if (!(file.ContentLength > 0)) return "";

        string fileName = file.FileName;
        string fileExt = Path.GetExtension(file.FileName);

        // Make sure we were able to determine a proper
        // extension
        if (null == fileExt) return "";

        // Check if the directory we are saving to exists
        if (!Directory.Exists(FilesPath))
        {
            // If it doesn't exist, create the directory
            Directory.CreateDirectory(FilesPath);
        }

        // Set our full path for saving
        string path = FilesPath + DirSeparator + fileName;

        // Save our file
        file.SaveAs(Path.GetFullPath(path));

        // Return the filename
        return fileName;
    }

    public static void DeleteFile(string fileName)
    {
        // Don't do anything if there is no name
        if (fileName.Length == 0) return;

        // Set our full path for deleting
        string path = FilesPath + DirSeparator + fileName;

        // Check if our file exists
        if (File.Exists(Path.GetFullPath(path)))
        {
            // Delete our file
            File.Delete(Path.GetFullPath(path));
        }
    }

}
}
```

The class and functions inside are defined as static to avoid the need to instantiate the class in the `BooksController`. At the top of the class, a constant is created that defines where files will be saved—this should be updated as needed to save in a different location on your website. In the `UploadFile` function, if the directory of where files will be uploaded doesn't already exist, it will be created using the `CreateDirectory` function from the `System.IO.Directory` class. A similar check is done in the delete function to make sure the file exists before deleting it with the `File.Delete` function. If this check is not performed, an error would be returned if the function attempted to delete a file that does not exist.

Finally the `BooksController` needs to be updated. In the following example, three important changes are done:

1. The `Create` function is updated to call the `UploadFile` function.
2. The `Edit` function is updated to first call the `DeleteFile` function, then call the `UploadFile` function.
3. The `DeleteConfirmed` function is updated to call the `DeleteFile` function before deleting the book from the database.

```
using System;
using System.Collections.Generic;
using System.Data;
using System.Data.Entity;
using System.Linq;
using System.Linq.Dynamic;
using System.Web;
using System.Web.Mvc;
using MvcApplication4.Models;
using MvcApplication4.Utils;
using PagedList;

namespace MvcApplication4.Controllers
{
    public class BooksController : Controller
    {
        private BookDBContext db = new BookDBContext();

        ...

        //
        // GET: /Books/Create

        public ActionResult Create()
        {
            return View();
        }

        //
        // POST: /Books/Create

        [HttpPost]
```

```csharp
public ActionResult Create(Book book,
        HttpPostedFileBase file)
{
    if (ModelState.IsValid)
    {
        // Upload our file
        book.Thumbnail = FileUpload.UploadFile(file);

        db.Books.Add(book);
        db.SaveChanges();
        return RedirectToAction("Index");
    }

    return View(book);
}

//
// GET: /Books/Edit/5

public ActionResult Edit(int id)
{
    Book book = db.Books.Find(id);
    return View(book);
}

//
// POST: /Books/Edit/5

[HttpPost]
public ActionResult Edit(Book book,
        HttpPostedFileBase file)
{
    if (ModelState.IsValid)
    {
        // Delete old file
        FileUpload.DeleteFile(book.Thumbnail);

        // Upload our file
        book.Thumbnail = FileUpload.UploadFile(file);

        db.Entry(book).State = EntityState.Modified;
        db.SaveChanges();
        return RedirectToAction("Index");
    }
    return View(book);
}

//
// GET: /Books/Delete/5

public ActionResult Delete(int id)
{
    Book book = db.Books.Find(id);
    return View(book);
}
```

```
//
// POST: /Books/Delete/5

[HttpPost, ActionName("Delete")]
public ActionResult DeleteConfirmed(int id)
{
    Book book = db.Books.Find(id);

    // Delete old file
    FileUpload.DeleteFile(book.Thumbnail);

    db.Books.Remove(book);
    db.SaveChanges();
    return RedirectToAction("Index");
}

    ...
  }
}
```

See Also

HttpPostedFileBase (*http://msdn.microsoft.com/en-us/library/system.web.httppostedfile base.aspx*)

1.12 Resizing an Image to Create a Thumbnail

Problem

You allow a user to upload an image, but typically this will be from a camera with pictures that are quite large, so you want to display a sample or thumbnail of the image on your website, allowing the user to preview the image before seeing the full image.

Solution

Update the existing file upload to resize an image with the following classes: File Stream, Image, Bitmap, and Graphics class to a specific width and height.

Discussion

In the following example, the previously created FileUpload class will be updated and reorganized. A new function called ResizeImage is created to perform the resizing. The resized image will be saved in a subfolder of where the previous files were saved, called Thumbnails. The DeleteFile function is also updated to remove both the thumbnail and original image, and a new function is created and called twice from the delete function to avoid duplicating code. The partial file upload class is displayed below, identifying the changes:

```csharp
using System;
using System.Collections.Generic;
using System.Linq;
using System.Web;
using System.IO;
using System.Drawing;
using System.Drawing.Drawing2D;

namespace MvcApplication4.Utils
{
    public static class FileUpload
    {
        public static char DirSeparator =
            System.IO.Path.DirectorySeparatorChar;
        public static string FilesPath = "Content" +
            DirSeparator + "Uploads" + DirSeparator;

        public static string UploadFile(HttpPostedFileBase file)
        {
            ...

            // Save our thumbnail as well
            ResizeImage(file, 150, 100);

            ...
        }

        public static void DeleteFile(string fileName)
        {
            // Don't do anything if there is no name
            if (fileName.Length == 0) return;

            // Set our full path for deleting
            string path = FilesPath + DirSeparator + fileName;
            string thumbPath = FilesPath + DirSeparator +
                "Thumbnails" + DirSeparator + fileName;

            RemoveFile(path);
            RemoveFile(thumbPath);
        }

        private static void RemoveFile(string path)
        {
            // Check if our file exists
            if (File.Exists(Path.GetFullPath(path)))
            {
                // Delete our file
                File.Delete(Path.GetFullPath(path));
            }
        }

        public static void ResizeImage(HttpPostedFileBase file,
            int width, int height)
        {
```

```csharp
string thumbnailDirectory =
    String.Format(@"{0}{1}{2}", FilesPath,
        DirSeparator, "Thumbnails");

// Check if the directory we are saving to exists
if (!Directory.Exists(thumbnailDirectory))
{
    // If it doesn't exist, create the directory
    Directory.CreateDirectory(thumbnailDirectory);
}

// Final path we will save our thumbnail
string imagePath =
    String.Format(@"{0}{1}{2}", thumbnailDirectory,
        DirSeparator, file.FileName);
// Create a stream to save the file to when we're
// done resizing
FileStream stream = new FileStream(Path.GetFullPath(
    imagePath), FileMode.OpenOrCreate);

// Convert our uploaded file to an image
Image OrigImage = Image.FromStream(file.InputStream);
// Create a new bitmap with the size of our
// thumbnail
Bitmap TempBitmap = new Bitmap(width, height);

// Create a new image that contains quality
// information
Graphics NewImage = Graphics.FromImage(TempBitmap);
NewImage.CompositingQuality =
    CompositingQuality.HighQuality;
NewImage.SmoothingMode =
    SmoothingMode.HighQuality;
NewImage.InterpolationMode =
    InterpolationMode.HighQualityBicubic;

// Create a rectangle and draw the image
Rectangle imageRectangle = new Rectangle(0, 0,
    width, height);
NewImage.DrawImage(OrigImage, imageRectangle);

// Save the final file
TempBitmap.Save(stream, OrigImage.RawFormat);

// Clean up the resources
NewImage.Dispose();
TempBitmap.Dispose();
OrigImage.Dispose();
stream.Close();
stream.Dispose();
            }
        }
    }
```

A lot is happening in the above example, specifically in the ResizeImage function. Firstly, if the Thumbnails directory doesn't already exist, it will be created. Next, a new FileStream is created for editing with the full path to where the final thumbnail will be saved.

Then the original uploaded image is converted to an object of the Image class using the InputStream of the uploaded file. A new Bitmap image is created based on the width and height of the thumbnail that will be created. This Bitmap image is then used to create a new Graphics object. The Graphics object, NewImage, is then used to set and define the quality, smooth, interpolation mode. Without these settings, the thumbnail image would not look good and be extremely pixelated and resized awkwardly.

Once this is all set, a new Rectangle is created and the original image is drawn to the Graphics object. This is what performs the actually resizing. Finally the Bitmap is saved and all of the objects created are disposed of, to free up resources.

 In the above example, a few important things (that should be updated before using in production) have been left out to focus on the resizing of the image. They are: validating that the uploaded file is an image; and checking the orientation of the original image to create a thumbnail that is not a fixed size of 150 pixels by 150 pixels, but resized to contain a constant width and allowing the height to be calculated to match the original orientation.

See Also

FileStream (*http://msdn.microsoft.com/en-us/library/system.io.filestream.aspx*), Image (*http://msdn.microsoft.com/en-us/library/system.drawing.image.aspx*), Bitmap (*http://msdn.microsoft.com/en-us/library/system.drawing.bitmap.aspx*), and Graphics (*http://msdn.microsoft.com/en-us/library/system.drawing.graphics.aspx*)

1.13 Implementing Ajax to Enhance the User Experience

Problem

When you click a link and the full web page is reloaded with the updated content, this can feel like a slow process, especially when only a small amount of the content is being updated.

Solution

Update previously created Html.ActionLink calls to use the Ajax helper and the Ajax.ActionLink to only reload the content being changed.

Discussion

MVC provides several great helper classes. So far throughout this book, the HTML helper class has been used extensively. In all of the views created, it was used at least once in each of them. In this recipe, the HTML helper class will be swapped out in the Books/Index view and replaced with the Ajax helper class.

Implementing Ajax requires a bit of additional setup before it can be used. Oftentimes I have found that this additional work can deter developers from using it. Let it be known that the additional setup time required is well worth it, because the benefits gained in the user experience are well worth the effort.

The setup starts with the Web.config file. Two keys must be set to true, ClientValidationEnabled and UnobtrusiveJavaScriptEnabled:

```
<?xml version="1.0"?>
<configuration>
  <connectionStrings>
    <add name="ApplicationServices" connectionString=
        "data source=.\SQLEXPRESS;Integrated Security=SSPI;
        AttachDBFilename=|DataDirectory|aspnetdb.mdf;
        User Instance=true" providerName="System.Data.SqlClient"/>
  </connectionStrings>

  <appSettings>
    <add key="webpages:Version" value="1.0.0.0" />
    <add key="ClientValidationEnabled" value="true" />
    <add key="UnobtrusiveJavaScriptEnabled" value="true" />
    <add key="smtpServer" value="localhost" />
    <add key="smtpPort" value="25" />
    <add key="smtpUser" value="" />
    <add key="smtpPass" value="" />
  </appSettings>

  <system.web>
    <compilation debug="true" targetFramework="4.0">
      <assemblies>
        <add assembly="System.Web.Abstractions,
                Version=4.0.0.0, Culture=neutral,
                PublicKeyToken=31BF3856AD364E35" />
        <add assembly="System.Web.Helpers,
                Version=1.0.0.0, Culture=neutral,
                PublicKeyToken=31BF3856AD364E35" />
        <add assembly="System.Web.Routing,
                Version=4.0.0.0, Culture=neutral,
                PublicKeyToken=31BF3856AD364E35" />
        <add assembly="System.Web.Mvc,
                Version=3.0.0.0, Culture=neutral,
                PublicKeyToken=31BF3856AD364E35" />
        <add assembly="System.Web.WebPages,
                Version=1.0.0.0, Culture=neutral,
                PublicKeyToken=31BF3856AD364E35" />
```

```
          <add assembly="System.Data.Entity,
                Version=4.0.0.0, Culture=neutral,
                PublicKeyToken=b77a5c561934e089" />
        </assemblies>
      </compilation>

    ...
  </system.web>

  ...
</configuration>
```

The final setup step that needs to be completed is to include several JavaScript files. This will be done in the shared layout that is used by all of the views created to date. In Views/Shared/_Layout.cshtml, two JavaScript files have been included in the <head> tag:

```
<!DOCTYPE html>
<html>
<head>
    <title>@ViewBag.Title</title>
    <link href="@Url.Content("~/Content/Site.css")"
        rel="stylesheet" type="text/css" />
    <script src="@Url.Content("~/Scripts/jquery-1.5.1.min.js")"
        type="text/javascript"></script>
    <script src="
        @Url.Content("~/Scripts/jquery.unobtrusive-ajax.min.js")"
            type="text/javascript"></script>
</head>
<body>
    <div class="page">
        <div id="header">
            <div id="title">
                <h1>My MVC Application</h1>
            </div>
            <div id="logindisplay">
                @Html.Partial("_LogOnPartial")
                [ @Html.ActionLink("English", "ChangeLanguage",
                    "Home", new { language = "en" }, null) ]
                [ @Html.ActionLink("Français", "ChangeLanguage",
                    "Home", new { language = "fr" }, null) ]
            </div>
            <div id="menucontainer">
                <ul id="menu">
                    <li>
                        @Html.ActionLink("Home", "Index", "Home")
                    </li>
                    <li>
                        @Html.ActionLink("About", "About", "Home")
                    </li>
                </ul>
            </div>
        </div>
```

```
        <div id="main">
            @RenderBody()
        </div>
        <div id="footer">
        </div>
    </div>
</body>
</html>
```

These files are automatically included in the base MVC 3 application. That completes the core of the Ajax setup. Next, the `Books/Index` view will be updated. In the following example, the three filter links and sortable header links have been updated to use the `Ajax.ActionLink` instead of the `Html.ActionLink`:

```
@model PagedList.IPagedList<MvcApplication4.Models.Book>

@if (IsAjax)
{
    Layout = null;
}

<h2>@MvcApplication4.Resources.Resource1.BookIndexTitle</h2>

<p>
    @Html.ActionLink("Create New", "Create")
</p>
<p>
    Show:
    @if (ViewBag.CurrentFilter != "")
    {
        @Ajax.ActionLink("All", "Index", new {
                sortOrder = ViewBag.CurrentSortOrder,
                Keyword = ViewBag.CurrentKeyword },
                new AjaxOptions { UpdateTargetId = "main" })
    }
    else
    {
        @:All
    }
      |  
    @if (ViewBag.CurrentFilter != "NewReleases")
    {
        @Ajax.ActionLink("New Releases", "Index", new {
                filter = "NewReleases",
                sortOrder = ViewBag.CurrentSortOrder,
                Keyword = ViewBag.CurrentKeyword },
                new AjaxOptions { UpdateTargetId = "main" })
    }
    else
    {
        @:New Releases
    }
      |  
    @if (ViewBag.CurrentFilter != "ComingSoon")
```

```
        {
            @Ajax.ActionLink("Coming Soon", "Index", new {
                    filter = "ComingSoon",
                    sortOrder = ViewBag.CurrentSortOrder,
                    Keyword = ViewBag.CurrentKeyword },
                    new AjaxOptions { UpdateTargetId = "main" })
        }
        else
        {
            @:Coming Soon
        }
    </p>
    @using (Html.BeginForm())
    {
        @:Search: @Html.TextBox("Keyword")
        <input type="submit" value="Search" />
    }
    @Html.Partial("_Paging")
    <table>
        <tr>
            <th>
                @Ajax.ActionLink("Title", "Index", new {
                    sortOrder = ViewBag.TitleSortParam,
                    filter = ViewBag.CurrentFilter,
                    Keyword = ViewBag.CurrentKeyword },
                    new AjaxOptions { UpdateTargetId = "main" })
            </th>
            <th>
                @Ajax.ActionLink("Isbn", "Index", new {
                    sortOrder = ViewBag.IsbnSortParam,
                    filter = ViewBag.CurrentFilter,
                    Keyword = ViewBag.CurrentKeyword },
                    new AjaxOptions { UpdateTargetId = "main" })
            </th>
            <th>
                Summary
            </th>
            <th>
                @Ajax.ActionLink("Author", "Index", new {
                    sortOrder = ViewBag.AuthorSortParam,
                    filter = ViewBag.CurrentFilter,
                    Keyword = ViewBag.CurrentKeyword },
                    new AjaxOptions { UpdateTargetId = "main" })
            </th>
            <th>
                Thumbnail
            </th>
            <th>
                @Ajax.ActionLink("Price", "Index", new {
                    sortOrder = ViewBag.PriceSortParam,
                    filter = ViewBag.CurrentFilter,
                    Keyword = ViewBag.CurrentKeyword },
                    new AjaxOptions { UpdateTargetId = "main" })
            </th>
```

```
        <th>
            @Ajax.ActionLink("Published", "Index", new {
                sortOrder = ViewBag.PublishedSortParam,
                filter = ViewBag.CurrentFilter,
                Keyword = ViewBag.CurrentKeyword },
                new AjaxOptions { UpdateTargetId = "main" })
        </th>
        <th></th>
    </tr>

@foreach (var item in Model)
{
    <tr>
        <td>
            @Html.DisplayFor(modelItem => item.Title)
        </td>
        <td>
            @Html.DisplayFor(modelItem => item.Isbn)
        </td>
        <td>
            @Html.DisplayFor(modelItem => item.Summary)
        </td>
        <td>
            @Html.DisplayFor(modelItem => item.Author)
        </td>
        <td>
            @Html.DisplayFor(modelItem => item.Thumbnail)
        </td>
        <td>
            @Html.DisplayFor(modelItem => item.Price)
        </td>
        <td>
            @Html.DisplayFor(modelItem => item.Published)
        </td>
        <td>
            @Html.ActionLink("Edit",
                "Edit", new { id = item.ID }) |
            @Html.ActionLink("Details",
                "Details", new { id = item.ID }) |
            @Html.ActionLink("Delete",
                "Delete", new { id = item.ID })
        </td>
    </tr>
}

</table>

@Html.Partial("_Paging")
```

The key thing that was done is that new `AjaxOptions` were added as the last parameter of the `ActionLink` function. This means that when the Ajax link is clicked by the user, the results of the Ajax request should update the HTML element with the `id` of `main`. If you look in the shared layout altered earlier, you will notice that it contains a `<div>`

with the id of main. In fact, this `<div>` is the container for the `@RenderBody()` function which is where the output of a view goes.

The other important thing that was done is a check for Ajax done at the top of the view. If the request was completed via Ajax, the layout is set to null. This is an extremely important factor because if this isn't done, the results of the Ajax request will contain not only the results of the view, but the full layout as well, which would be placed inside of the layout again.

To finish off this example, the Shared/_Paging view will also be updated to use the Ajax helper as well:

```
<p>
    @if (Model.HasPreviousPage)
    {
        @Ajax.ActionLink("<< First", "Index", new {
                page = 1,
                sortOrder = ViewBag.CurrentSortOrder,
                filter = ViewBag.CurrentFilter,
                Keyword = ViewBag.CurrentKeyword },
                new AjaxOptions { UpdateTargetId = "main" })
        @Html.Raw(" ");
        @Ajax.ActionLink("< Prev", "Index", new {
                page = Model.PageNumber - 1,
                sortOrder = ViewBag.CurrentSortOrder,
                filter = ViewBag.CurrentFilter,
                Keyword = ViewBag.CurrentKeyword },
                new AjaxOptions { UpdateTargetId = "main" })
    }
    else
    {
        @:<< First
        @Html.Raw(" ");
        @:< Prev
    }

      

    @if (Model.HasNextPage)
    {
        @Ajax.ActionLink("Next >", "Index", new {
                page = Model.PageNumber + 1,
                sortOrder = ViewBag.CurrentSortOrder,
                filter = ViewBag.CurrentFilter,
                Keyword = ViewBag.CurrentKeyword },
                new AjaxOptions { UpdateTargetId = "main" })
        @Html.Raw(" ");
        @Ajax.ActionLink("Last >>", "Index", new {
                page = Model.PageCount,
                sortOrder = ViewBag.CurrentSortOrder,
                filter = ViewBag.CurrentFilter,
                Keyword = ViewBag.CurrentKeyword },
                new AjaxOptions { UpdateTargetId = "main" })
    }
```

```
        else
        {
            @:Next >
            @Html.Raw(" ")
            @:Last >>
        }
    </p>
```

Now when the user clicks on a link that changes the list of books, the full page is not reloaded and only the list of books is updated, providing a much better and faster user experience.

Also, if the client does not support JavaScript (e.g., when a search engine visits), the link will still function normally, allowing both a user with JavaScript disabled and the search engine to still access the content through a normal full page reload.

See Also

AjaxHelper (*http://msdn.microsoft.com/en-us/library/system.web.mvc.ajaxhelper.aspx*)

1.14 Submitting a Form with Ajax

Problem

You have a page that lists important detail and you want to allow the user to quickly and easily submit a form without reloading the whole page and losing their place on the website.

Solution

Using the `AjaxHelper`, create a new form that is submitted by Ajax and automatically updates the existing content with the newly submitted item.

Discussion

The following example is going to put several of the previous recipes together, to demonstrate how to allow users to submit a comment on a book without being redirected to different pages to both see the comments and submit their own comment.

To start with, a new model must be created that will store the comments for a book. With the `Models` folder selected, right-click and choose *Add→Class*. The name of the class will be `BookComment.cs`. This model will store the comment submitted about a specific book:

```
using System;
using System.Collections.Generic;
using System.Linq;
using System.Web;
using System.ComponentModel.DataAnnotations;
```

```
namespace MvcApplication4.Models
{
    public class BookComment
    {
        public int ID { get; set; }
        [Required]
        public string Comment { get; set; }
        public DateTime Created { get; set; }

        public int BookId { get; set; }
        public virtual Book Book { get; set; }
    }

}
```

Next, the previously created `BookDBContext` must be updated to contain a reference to this table. This class was previously created in the original `Book` model. At this point, it would make sense to create a new file specifically to store this class, as it might continue to grow in your project with future tables. Right-clicking on the `Models` folder again, select *Add→Class*. The name of this class will be `BookDBContext`:

```
using System;
using System.Collections.Generic;
using System.Linq;
using System.Web;
using System.Data.Entity;

namespace MvcApplication4.Models
{
    public class BookDBContext : DbContext
    {
        public DbSet<Book> Books { get; set; }
        public DbSet<BookComment> BookComments { get; set; }
    }
}
```

At this point, you should rebuild your application so that the newly created model will appear in the next step.

Once this class is created, you can remove it from the `Book` model class. Next, a new controller must be created that will perform the listing of comments and the ability to manage them. With the `Controllers` folder selected, *click Add→Controller*. The name of the controller will be `BookCommentsController.cs`. To minimize the typing required, the new controller will be scaffolded with the *Entity Framework*. For the Model Class, choose the newly created `BookComment` model. For the Data context class, choose the previously created `BookDBContext`. Select *Add* once all of the settings are chosen.

When you run the application the next time, you should receive an error indicating that the `BookDBContext` has changed since it was last used. To solve this, you must create an initializer for the `DBContext`. Because this is not a production website, the initializer is going to *drop and recreate the database*. To perform this, right-click on the `Models` folder and select *Add→Class*. This class will be called `BookInitializer.cs`:

```
using System;
using System.Collections.Generic;
using System.Linq;
using System.Web;
using System.Data.Entity;

namespace MvcApplication4.Models
{
    public class BookInitializer :
                DropCreateDatabaseIfModelChanges<BookDBContext>
    {
    }
}
```

Next the `Global.asax.cs` must be updated to call this `BookInitializer` on `Applica tion_Start`:

```
using System;
using System.Collections.Generic;
using System.Linq;
using System.Web;
using System.Web.Mvc;
using System.Web.Routing;
using MvcApplication4.Models;
using System.Data.Entity;
using System.Globalization;
using System.Threading;

namespace MvcApplication4
{

    public class MvcApplication : System.Web.HttpApplication
    {
        ...

        protected void Application_Start()
        {
            Database.SetInitializer<BookDBContext>(
                new BookInitializer());

            ...
        }

        ...

    }
}
```

The setup work is now all complete, and it's time to perform the necessary updates to allow users to comment on a book with Ajax. This process will be started with the `Books/Details` view, as this is the most logical spot to display comments about the book:

```
@model MvcApplication4.Models.Book

@{
    ViewBag.Title = "Details";
}
```

```
<h2>Details</h2>

<fieldset>
    <legend>Book</legend>

    <div class="display-label">Title</div>
    <div class="display-field">
        @Html.DisplayFor(model => model.Title)
    </div>

    <div class="display-label">Isbn</div>
    <div class="display-field">
        @Html.DisplayFor(model => model.Isbn)
    </div>

    <div class="display-label">Summary</div>
    <div class="display-field">
        @Html.DisplayFor(model => model.Summary)
    </div>

    <div class="display-label">Author</div>
    <div class="display-field">
        @Html.DisplayFor(model => model.Author)
    </div>

    <div class="display-label">Thumbnail</div>
    <div class="display-field">
        @Html.DisplayFor(model => model.Thumbnail)
    </div>

    <div class="display-label">Price</div>
    <div class="display-field">
        @Html.DisplayFor(model => model.Price)
    </div>

    <div class="display-label">Published</div>
    <div class="display-field">
        @Html.DisplayFor(model => model.Published)
    </div>
</fieldset>
<fieldset>
    <legend>Comments</legend>
    <div id="Comments">
        @{Html.RenderAction("Index", "BookComments",
            new { BookId = Model.ID });}
    </div>
</fieldset>
<p>
    @Html.ActionLink("Edit", "Edit", new { id=Model.ID }) |
    @Html.ActionLink("Back to List", "Index")
</p>
```

In the above example, a new <fieldset> has been added beneath the details of the book. Inside this <fieldset> a new <div> has been created with the id of Comments. Inside this

`<div>` an `Html.RenderAction` is performed to the `BookComments Index` function passing a parameter called `BookId` with the id of the current book.

Next, the `BookComments/Index` view needs to be updated. In the following example, the *Create New* link is updated to display the form via Ajax instead of redirecting the user to a new page. A new `<div>` has been placed right beneath this link, which will be used to populate the form when the Ajax call completes. A few links have been removed as well, because no comment managing will be provided—only the ability to add comments.

```
@model IEnumerable<MvcApplication4.Models.BookComment>

@{
    ViewBag.Title = "Index";
}

<h2>Index</h2>

<p>
    @Ajax.ActionLink("Create New", "Create", new {
            BookId = ViewBag.BookId },
            new AjaxOptions { UpdateTargetId = "AddComment" })
</p>
<div id="AddComment"></div>
<table>
    <tr>
        <th>
            Comment
        </th>
        <th>
            Created
        </th>
    </tr>

@foreach (var item in Model) {
    <tr>
        <td>
            @Html.DisplayFor(modelItem => item.Comment)
        </td>
        <td>
            @Html.DisplayFor(modelItem => item.Created)
        </td>
        <td>
            @Html.DisplayFor(modelItem => item.Book.Title)
        </td>
    </tr>
}

</table>
```

The final view that requires changes is the automatically generated `BookComments/Create` view. This view is updated to use the `Ajax.BeginForm` instead of the default `Html.BeginForm`. The other thing that is done is tell the form to call a JavaScript function called ReloadComments when the Ajax submit is completed. This function performs an Ajax request with JQuery to retrieve the updated comments list. A hidden form field was also created with the BookId instead of the automatically created drop-down list of books.

```
@model MvcApplication4.Models.BookComment

@{
    ViewBag.Title = "Create";
}

<h2>Create</h2>

<script src="@Url.Content("~/Scripts/jquery.validate.min.js")"
    type="text/javascript"></script>
<script src="
    @Url.Content("~/Scripts/jquery.validate.unobtrusive.min.js")"
    type="text/javascript"></script>
<script type="text/javascript">
    function ReloadComments() {
        $("#Comments").load("@Url.Content(
            "~/BookComments/Index?BookId=" + ViewBag.BookId)");
    }
</script>
@using (Ajax.BeginForm(new AjaxOptions {
        OnComplete="ReloadComments()" }))
{
    @Html.Hidden("BookId", (int)ViewBag.BookId);
    @Html.ValidationSummary(true)
    <fieldset>
        <legend>BookComment</legend>

        <div class="editor-label">
            @Html.LabelFor(model => model.Comment)
        </div>
        <div class="editor-field">
            @Html.EditorFor(model => model.Comment)
            @Html.ValidationMessageFor(model => model.Comment)
        </div>

        <p>
            <input type="submit" value="Create" />
        </p>
    </fieldset>
}
```

To complete this example, a few changes are required to the BookCommentsController:

```
using System;
using System.Collections.Generic;
using System.Data;
using System.Data.Entity;
using System.Linq;
using System.Web;
using System.Web.Mvc;
```

```
using MvcApplication4.Models;

namespace MvcApplication4.Controllers
{
    public class BookCommentsController : Controller
    {
        private BookDBContext db = new BookDBContext();

        //
        // GET: /BookComments/

        public ActionResult Index(int BookId)
        {
            ViewBag.BookId = BookId;
            var bookcomments = db.BookComments.Include(
                b => b.Book).Where(b => b.BookId == BookId);
            return PartialView(bookcomments.ToList());
        }

        //
        // GET: /BookComments/Create

        public ActionResult Create(int BookId)
        {
            ViewBag.BookId = BookId;
            return PartialView();
        }

        //
        // POST: /BookComments/Create

        [HttpPost]
        public ActionResult Create(BookComment bookcomment)
        {
            if (ModelState.IsValid)
            {
                bookcomment.Created = DateTime.Now;
                db.BookComments.Add(bookcomment);
                db.SaveChanges();
            }

            ViewBag.BookId = bookcomment.BookId;
            return PartialView(bookcomment);
        }

        protected override void Dispose(bool disposing)
        {
            db.Dispose();
            base.Dispose(disposing);
        }
    }
}
```

In the above example, the Index function has been updated to accept an integer for the BookId. This is set to the ViewBag. The other important change to this function is, instead of returning a full view, only a partial view is returned (preventing the full layout from being displayed). If you recall in the previous example, we reused the same view to perform the Ajax request, and had to check within the view to see if it was an Ajax request, to disable the layout. Since this view is only displayed via Ajax, it's simpler to update the controller to return a partial view.

Finally, the Create functions have been updated as well. The basic Create function has been updated just like the Index to accept a BookId and return a partial view. The second Create function has been updated to set the created date of the comment to *now*, and if there is an error, to return a partial view. The additional Edit, Details, and Delete functions have been removed since they are not being used. These views can also be deleted since they are not being used.

Now when a user is viewing the details of a book, they can see the list of comments already posted and if they wish to add their own comment, they can click the *Create New* link, enter their comment, click Submit, and automatically see their newly created comment without ever having to leave the book details page.

1.15 Enabling a CAPTCHA

Problem

Unfortunately there are people who use automated programs to submit forms, causing a lot of spam throughout the Internet. One of the ways to prevent this is to implement a CAPTCHA (an acronym for "Completely Automated Public Turing test to tell Computers and Humans Apart"), which forces users to type a generated word into a text box.

Solution

Install the *ASP.NET Web Helpers Library* from *NuGet* to integrate a CAPTCHA into the BookCommentsController.

Discussion

A new library package is required to enable a CAPTCHA on a form. Microsoft has created a NuGet Web Helpers library that contains a built in CAPTCHA class that easily let's us render and validate the CAPTCHA entered by the user.

With the MVC Application project selected in Visual Studio, click *Tools→Library Package Manager→Add Library Package Reference*. Once loaded, select the Online button on the left. On the first page, there should be a package called microsoft-web-helpers—if it is not there, try searching for it in the top right. Once found, click the *Install* button.

The most typical places where automated form submission software is used are comment submissions. Since in a previous recipe, comments on books were added, this is a perfect spot to add the CAPTCHA. Before starting, you must register your domain at the RECAPTCHA website (*http://www.google.com/recaptcha*). When you have completed registration, you will receive a public and private key for your domain. Copy and paste these somewhere for future use.

 If you are not using Ajax to include the CAPTCHA, you can simplify the view changes by simply adding the two following lines in your view:

```
@using Microsoft.Web.Helpers;

@ReCaptcha.GetHtml("<your_public_key>", "<your_private_key>")
```

With the setup complete, it's time to start updating the code. A small update must be made to the `BookComments/Index` view. This view was previously created to Ajax the create comment on the page. This Ajax request needs to be updated to display the CAPTCHA button, by calling the `DisplayCaptcha` JavaScript function when the request is complete.

```
@model IEnumerable<MvcApplication4.Models.BookComment>

@{
    ViewBag.Title = "Index";
}

<h2>Index</h2>

<p>
    @Ajax.ActionLink("Create New", "Create", new {
            BookId = ViewBag.BookId },
            new AjaxOptions { UpdateTargetId = "AddComment",
            OnComplete = "DisplayCaptcha" })
</p>
<div id="AddComment"></div>

...

<script type="text/javascript" src=
    "http://www.google.com/recaptcha/api/js/recaptcha_ajax.js">
</script>
<script type="text/javascript">
    function DisplayCaptcha() {
        Recaptcha.destroy();
        Recaptcha.create("<your_public_key>", "captcha", {});
    }
</script>
```

Now the `BookComments/Create` view needs to be updated in a similar fashion. First, a new spot needs to be created for the CAPTCHA to be displayed. Also, a new HTML error message is added to tell the user when they enter an incorrect caption. Finally, the ReloadComments JavaScript function is updated to not automatically reload the comments (only when there are no errors).

```
@model MvcApplication4.Models.BookComment
@{
    ViewBag.Title = "Create";
}

<h2>Create</h2>

@section JavascriptAndCSS {
<script src="@Url.Content("~/Scripts/jquery.validate.min.js")"
  type="text/javascript"></script>
<script src="
  @Url.Content("~/Scripts/jquery.validate.unobtrusive.min.js")"
    type="text/javascript"></script>
}

<script type="text/javascript">
    function ReloadComments() {
        var reload = "@ViewBag.RefreshComments";
        if (reload == "False") {
            DisplayCaptcha();
        } else {
            $("#Comments").load(
                "/BookComments/Index?BookId=@ViewBag.BookId");
        }
    }
</script>
@using (Ajax.BeginForm(new AjaxOptions {
    UpdateTargetId="AddComment", OnComplete="ReloadComments" }))
{
    @Html.Hidden("BookId", (int)ViewBag.BookId);
    @Html.ValidationSummary(true)
    <fieldset>
        <legend>BookComment</legend>

        <div class="editor-label">
            @Html.LabelFor(model => model.Comment)
        </div>
        <div class="editor-field">
            @Html.TextAreaFor(model => model.Comment)
            @Html.ValidationMessageFor(model => model.Comment)
        </div>

        <div class="editor-label">
            Are you human?
        </div>

        <div class="editor-field">
            <div id="captcha"></div>
            @Html.ValidationMessage("Captcha")
        </div>
```

```
      <p>
          <input type="submit" value="Create" />
      </p>
    </fieldset>
  }
```

Finally, the BookCommentsController needs to be updated to validate the CAPTCHA entered by the user. If the CAPTCHA is invalid, an error message is added to the ModelState so the view will display it properly.

```
using System;
using System.Collections.Generic;
using System.Data;
using System.Data.Entity;
using System.Linq;
using System.Web;
using System.Web.Mvc;
using MvcApplication4.Models;
using Microsoft.Web.Helpers;

namespace MvcApplication4.Controllers
{
    public class BookCommentsController : Controller
    {
        private BookDBContext db = new BookDBContext();

        //
        // GET: /BookComments/

        public ActionResult Index(int BookId)
        {
            ViewBag.BookId = BookId;
            var bookcomments = db.BookComments.Include(
                b => b.Book).Where(b => b.BookId == BookId);
            return PartialView(bookcomments.ToList());
        }

        //
        // GET: /BookComments/Create

        public ActionResult Create(int BookId)
        {
            ViewBag.BookId = BookId;
            ViewBag.RefreshComments = false;
            return PartialView();
        }

        //
        // POST: /BookComments/Create

        [HttpPost]
        public ActionResult Create(BookComment bookcomment)
        {
```

```
        ViewBag.RefreshComments = false;
        var captchaSuccess = ReCaptcha.Validate(
            "<your_private_key>");

        if (ModelState.IsValid && captchaSuccess)
        {
            bookcomment.Created = DateTime.Now;
            db.BookComments.Add(bookcomment);
            db.SaveChanges();

            ViewBag.RefreshComments = true;
        }

        // if captcha failed add error message
        if (!captchaSuccess)
        {
            ModelState.AddModelError("Captcha",
                "Invalid CAPTCHA");
        }

        ViewBag.BookId = bookcomment.BookId;
        return PartialView(bookcomment);
    }

    protected override void Dispose(bool disposing)
    {
        db.Dispose();
        base.Dispose(disposing);
    }
  }
}
```

1.16 Mobilizing Your Website

Problem

By default, your website probably won't display well on a mobile device. Granted, some devices are good enough to make it fit on the phone, but it won't be fluid and you probably don't want to build a whole new website for a mobile phone, as that becomes costly.

Solution

Using the *JQuery Mobile NuGet* package, alter the shared layout and views and make a website that will look good both on a traditional browser *and* most mobile phones.

Discussion

First and foremost, if you have been reading the roadmap regarding MVC 4, you will have noticed a lot of discussion around mobile enhancements—specifically the adaptation of using the JQuery Mobile toolkit that will be used in this example.

Unfortunately, at this time it's too early to tell how far this will be taken in MVC 4, as a lot of things indicate that we "might" provide it. So instead of waiting for it, I will provide an extremely straightforward solution that requires minimal effort to maintain both a mobile web application and a regular web application. Furthermore, with Windows 8 coming out soon and support for HTML5 web applications right on the desktop, it will also be a desktop application.

Maintaining multiple versions of the same website does come with risks and additional time requirements. Each time you add new functionality, you must firstly test the new functionality in the multiple environments, as well as regression test in the multiple environments. Also, just because this is considered "straightforward" doesn't mean that it's mindless: a lot of thought must be given to the organization of the page structure to ensure it's built as best as possible for both major platforms: desktop browser and mobile browser.

To begin with, the *JQuery Mobile* package needs to be added through the *NuGet* package manager. With the current build of MVC 3, JQuery 1.5.x is included by default with the application. The current version of JQuery Mobile depends on version 1.6.x, so the versions of JQuery must be updated. Luckily the *NuGet* package manager has created a simple way to perform this.

With the MVC Application project selected, *click Tools→Library Package Manager→Add Library Package Reference*. Instead of adding the JQuery Mobile package, the existing JQuery packages must be updated. On the left, select the *Update* button. This will contain a list of the currently installed packages that have been updated. Before updating the base JQuery package, several of its child packages must be updated first.

If you receive any errors while updating any of the packages because of reference issues, be sure to read the versions indicated and try updating those packages first.

I found the following order to work successfully (click each and then select *Update*, then move on to the next): *Jquery.Validation*, *Jquery.vs.doc*, *Jquery.ui.combined*, and finally the *JQuery* package itself.

Several changes have occurred between JQuery 1.5.x and JQuery 1.6.x, so before updating your version, please read the changelog to ensure that your existing code will not cease to function because of the upgrade.

Once all the package updates have been performed, you can now click on the *Online* button from the left menu. In the search box, type `Jquery.Mobile` and click *Install*. This will install the necessary CSS and JavaScript files required to use the JQuery add-on.

The JQuery Mobile plugin is based on HTML5 syntax. Using this syntax, various CSS and JavaScript manipulations are done within the page to provide the desired look that closely matches built-in applications on some of the more popular smartphones.

The purpose of this example is demonstrate how an existing website can be updated to use this new library and still maintain a web version as well as a mobile version. To begin, the Shared/_Layout view needs to be updated to match the JQuery Mobile page anatomy syntax.

```
<!DOCTYPE html>

<html>
<head>
    <title>@ViewBag.Title</title>
    <link href="@Url.Content(
        "~/Content/jquery.mobile-1.0b1.min.css")"
            rel="stylesheet" type="text/css" />
    <script src="@Url.Content("~/Scripts/jquery-1.6.2.min.js")"
        type="text/javascript"></script>

    <script type="text/javascript">
        $(document).ready(function () {
            if (window.innerWidth > 480) {
                $("link[rel=stylesheet]").attr({ href:
                    "@Url.Content("~/Content/Site.css")" });
            }
        });
    </script>

    <script src="@Url.Content(
        "~/Scripts/jquery.mobile-1.0b1.min.js")"
            type="text/javascript"></script>

    @RenderSection("JavaScriptAndCSS", required: false)
</head>
<body>
    <div class="page" data-role="page">
        <div id="header" data-role="header">
            <div id="title">
                <h1>My MVC Application</h1>
            </div>
            <div id="logindisplay" class="ui-bar">
                @Html.Partial("_LogOnPartial")
                [ @Html.ActionLink("English", "ChangeLanguage",
                    "Home", new { language = "en" }, null) ]
                [ @Html.ActionLink("Français", "ChangeLanguage",
                    "Home", new { language = "fr" }, null) ]
            </div>
            <div id="menucontainer" class="ui-bar">
                <ul id="menu">
                    <li>@Html.ActionLink("Home", "Index", "Home",
                        null, new Dictionary<string, object>
                            {{ "data-role", "button" }})</li>
```

```
            <li>@Html.ActionLink("About", "About", "Home",
                null, new Dictionary<string, object>
                    {{ "data-role", "button" }})</li>
            </ul>
        </div>
    </div>
    <div id="main" data-role="content">
        @RenderBody()
    </div>
    <div id="footer" data-role="footer">
    </div>
    </div>
</body>
</html>
```

Hopefully the above example looks pretty similar to you. This is the shared layouts' base HTML as was created with the project template. To make it function for JQuery Mobile, the following things have been done:

1. Included the JQuery Mobile CSS file

2. Included the JQuery Mobile JavaScript file

3. Added multiple `data-role` attributes to the existing `<div>` tags that contained the page, header, content, and footer elements, as well as several other classes and data-role for menu affects

4. Added some JavaScript detection to swap out the CSS if the browser size is greater than 480 pixels, to include the default CSS

There are several ways to accomplish the last item (e.g., use the `@media` tag in CSS to target screen sizes, perform phone and browser detection, and so on). Based on your needs you will need to determine what's the best solution. Maybe your website should perform some sort of detection, or perhaps even web browsers should use the mobile template—it's up to you.

If you were to run the application twice (once in full screen mode, and once on your mobile device or by simply resizing the browser below 480 pixels), you will see two very different websites (see Figures 1-6 and 1-7).

As you can tell, there is still a lot of work to be done to make everything look good, but by adding a few additional `data-role` attributes to the default layout, 90% of the work has been completed already. The next steps are exploring particular features that are of interest for your website. JQuery Mobile has full functionality for the following basic smartphone features:

• Navbars (in header or footer, with or without icons)

• Page transitions

• Dialogs

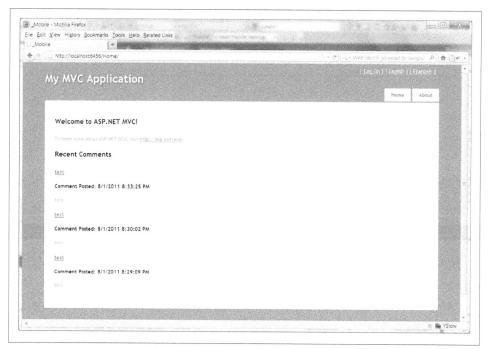

Figure 1-6. Default MVC template

- Buttons
- Forms
- List views (that provide the typical finger scrolling on the mobile platform)
- Full theming support to swap out the complete look-and-feel

Example Navbars:

```
<div id="logindisplay" class="ui-bar">
    @Html.Partial("_LogOnPartial")
    @Html.ActionLink("English", "ChangeLanguage", "Home",
            new { language = "en" }, null) ]
    @Html.ActionLink("Français", "ChangeLanguage", "Home",
            new { language = "fr" }, null) ]
</div>
```

The following example will render typical smartphone-looking buttons, and additional links will all be added with the same style.

Example Page Transition:

```
@Html.ActionLink("My Cool Link", "SomeAction", "Home", null,
            new Dictionary<string, object>
            {{ "data-transition", "slide" }})
```

The following page transition will slide in the new content once the link has been loaded via Ajax. In our standard website, this would work as every other link currently does.

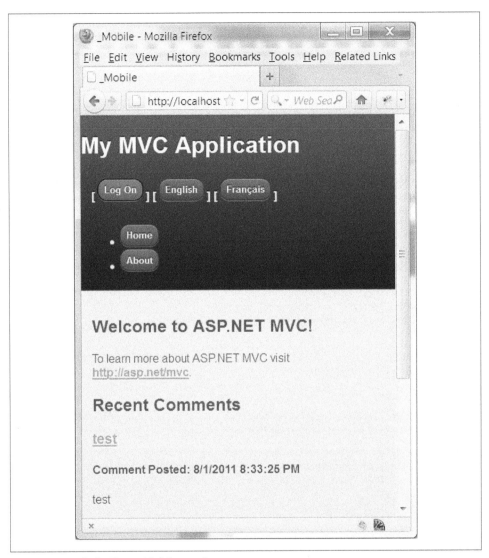

Figure 1-7. Default JQuery Mobile template

Example Dialog:

```
@Html.ActionLink("My Cool Link", "SomeAction", "Home", null,
            new Dictionary<string, object>
            {{ "data-rel", "dialog" }})
```

Just like the previous example, this will render a generic link for a web browser, but in the mobile version, the standard popup would be displayed.

Example Button:

```
<div data-role="page">
    <div data-role="header">
        @Html.ActionLink("Cancel", "SomeAction", "Home", null,
                new Dictionary<string, object>
                {{ "data-icon", "delete" }})
        <h1>Page Title</h1>
        @Html.ActionLink("Save", "SomeAction", "Home", null,
                new Dictionary<string, object>
                {{ "data-icon", "check" }})
    </div>
</div>
```

As you might expect because these buttons are placed within the header, they will be rendered in the top bar, one on the left and one on the right, mimicking standard header button functionality in smartphones today.

Example Form Item:

```
<div class="editor-label">
    @Html.LabelFor(model => model.ShortName)
</div>
<div class="editor-field">
    @Html.EditorFor(model => model.ShortName)
    @Html.ValidationMessageFor(model => model.ShortName)
</div>
```

There is no change required. Most of the built-in form functionality will render exactly as expected with JQuery Mobile.

Example List View:

```
<ul data-role="listview" data-inset="true">
    <li data-role="list-divider">Books</li>
    @foreach (var item in Model)
    {
        <li>@Html.ActionLink(
                item.Title, "Details", new { id = item.ID })
        </li>
    }
</ul>
```

The above example will list all of the books, with their title set up as a link to the details page in a standard scrollable list.

Changing Theme Example:

Currently, JQuery Mobile contains five built-in themes, lettered from a through e. Each of the above items can have their theme changed by appending a new attribute called data-theme with a different letter (a through e).

See Also

JQuery Mobile (*http://jquerymobile.com/*)

1.17 Paging Through Content Without the Pages

Problem

A lot of websites today interact with a database. If your website receives a lot of traffic, the SQL queries to retrieve the data can be quite intense. More importantly because the average user clicks a link within 15 seconds of arriving at your website, the work to retrieve and generate the content might be unnecessary, especially when the content is "below the fold" (not visible without scrolling first). To help solve this issue, content will be loaded "on-demand". Enough content will be loaded to make the page feel populated and as the user scrolls down to read it, more content will be populated behind the scenes without affecting the user experience.

Solution

Using Asynchronous controllers along with JQuery to load a specific amount of upfront content and then load further content on-demand when the user begins scrolling through the website content.

Discussion

Asynchronous controllers are probably underused in many MVC applications to date—most likely because people don't know about them, or more importantly, don't know when to use them. The following is an excerpt from the MSDN site listed in the See Also section:

> "In applications where thread starvation might occur, you can configure actions to be processed asynchronously. An asynchronous request takes the same amount of time to process as a synchronous request. For example, if a request makes a network call that requires two seconds to complete, the request takes two seconds whether it is performed synchronously or asynchronously. However, during an asynchronous call, the server is not blocked from responding to other requests while it waits for the first request to complete. Therefore, asynchronous requests prevent request queuing when there are many requests that invoke long-running operations."

In this example, using Asynchronous requests is the perfect solution because it will free up IIS to serve more important requests, such as a new user arriving at the site for the first time. Where as, loading on-demand content for a user is less important because most people won't even notice the additional content being loaded.

In a typical social website, a user's comments are most likely to contain the most activity. In a previous recipe, the ability to comment on a book was created. In this example, the homepage of the site will be updated to list the most recent comments. Enough comments will be displayed so that scroll bars will appear. Once the user begins scrolling, an Ajax request to an asynchronous controller will be made to retrieve additional comments.

To begin, the Home/Index view must be updated to display the most recent comments. To provide some context around the comment, basic details about the book will also be displayed with links to view the book. A new controller will be created to display the comments, so this view will simply call the render function of the view to be created further down.

```
@model IEnumerable<MvcApplication4.Models.BookComment>

@{
    ViewBag.Title = "Home Page";
}

<h2>@ViewBag.Message</h2>
<p>
    To learn more about ASP.NET MVC visit
                <a href="http://asp.net/mvc"
                title="ASP.NET MVC Website">
                http://asp.net/mvc</a>.
</p>

<script type="text/javascript">
var lastY = 0;
var currentY = 0;
var page = 1;
var maxPages = @ViewBag.maxPages;

$(window).scroll(function () {
    if (page < maxPages) {
        currentY = $(window).scrollTop();
        if (currentY - lastY > 200 * (page - 1)) {
            lastY = currentY;
            page++;
            $.get('CommentFeed/Comments?page=' + page,
                function(data) {
                    $('#comments').append(data);
            });
        }
    }
});
</script>

<div id="comments">
    <h2>Recent Comments</h2>
    @Html.Partial("../CommentFeed/Comments", Model)
</div>
```

In the above example, there is also some relatively complex JavaScript code that is executed when the window is scrolled. Several global JavaScript variables are defined to keep track of the current "y" scroll location, the last "y" scroll location, and the current page being retrieved. When the window's scrollTop position minus the last scroll location is greater than a specific number, new book comments are retrieved through Ajax and appended to the list of comments. For your own website, you will need to adjust the number of pixels that works best, based on the height of the content, to ensure that new content is always retrieved in advance.

Next, the `HomeController` needs updating to retrieve the list of book comments. The comments are ordered by the created date in descending order to ensure the newest comments are displayed first. To prevent intense database load, the list of comments will be reduced to a small number. This should be adjusted on your website to ensure there is just enough content to cause scrollbars. In the example below, the comments are limited to 3. The maximum number of pages is also determined by dividing the total count of comments by 3. The max pages are used to prevent further Ajax calls once the maximum comments have been returned.

```
using System;
using System.Collections.Generic;
using System.Linq;
using System.Web;
using System.Web.Mvc;
using System.Globalization;
using System.Data.Entity;
using MvcApplication4.Models;

namespace MvcApplication4.Controllers
{
    public class HomeController : Controller
    {
        private BookDBContext db = new BookDBContext();

        public ActionResult Index()
        {
            ViewBag.Message = "Welcome to ASP.NET MVC!";

            // Get our recent comments
            var bookcomments = db.BookComments.Include(
                b => b.Book).OrderByDescending(b => b.Created).
                  Take(3);
            var count = db.BookComments.Count();
            ViewBag.maxPages =  count / 3 + 1;

            return View(bookcomments);
        }

        ...

    }
}
```

This same functionality needs to be duplicated into a new asynchronous controller. With the `Controllers` folder selected, right-click and *select Add→Controller*. The new controller will be called `CommentFeedController`. This controller doesn't need the scaffolded functions, so under the *Template* drop-down, change the selection to *Empty controller* and press *Add*.

This controller will look slightly different than a typical controller. With asynchronous controllers, one view is split into two functions. The first function performs the asynchronous request (e.g., retrieve the comments). The second function receives the results of the asynchronous call and returns or displays the results.

 In the following example, a partial view is rendered. In some applications, it might be beneficial to reduce the network traffic, return a JSON result, and let the JavaScript code deal with the display. However, to simplify this example and focus on asynchronous controllers, the former will be used and a partial view is returned.

```
using System;
using System.Collections.Generic;
using System.Linq;
using System.Web;
using System.Web.Mvc;
using MvcApplication4.Models;
using System.Data.Entity;

namespace MvcApplication4.Controllers
{
    public class CommentFeedController : AsyncController
    {
        private BookDBContext db = new BookDBContext();

        public void CommentsAsync(int page)
        {
            AsyncManager.OutstandingOperations.Increment();
            AsyncManager.Sync(() =>
            {
                var bookcomments = db.BookComments.Include(
                    b => b.Book).OrderByDescending(b =>
                        b.Created).Skip(page * 3).Take(3);
                AsyncManager.Parameters["bookcomments"] =
                    bookcomments;
                AsyncManager.OutstandingOperations.Decrement();
            });
        }

        public ActionResult CommentsCompleted(
                IEnumerable<BookComment> bookcomments)
        {
            return PartialView(bookcomments);
        }

    }
}
```

The first function, CommentsAsync, receives the current page passed in from JavaScript and uses this value to retrieve the next three comments. The first thing that happens is that the outstanding operations are incremented. Then through the Sync method, the comments are retrieved and passed as a variable to the second function. The final thing that happens is that the outstanding operations is decremented. It's important that the increment and decrement counter match; otherwise, the sync manager will cancel the request after a certain period of time when they do not match, to prevent never-ending requests.

The second function receives the book comments and returns a partial view. This is the same partial view that is called from the Home/Index view. The final step in this process is to create the partial view. Begin by right-clicking on the Views folder and *select Add→New Folder*. This folder should be called CommentFeed to match the controller name. Then with this folder selected, right-click and *select Add→View*. The view will be called Comments—be sure to check the *Partial View* before adding it.

```
@model IEnumerable<MvcApplication4.Models.BookComment>

@foreach (var item in Model) {
 <h3><a href="@Url.Action("Details", "Books", new {
              ID=item.Book.ID } )">
              @Html.DisplayFor(modelItem => item.Book.Title)
              </a></h3>
 <h4>Comment Posted: @Html.DisplayFor(
              modelItem => item.Created)</h4>
 <p>@MvcHtmlString.Create(Html.Encode(item.Comment).Replace(
              Environment.NewLine, "<br />"))</p>
}
```

The following view loops through the comments and first displays the title of the book and links to the details page of it, then the date the comment was created, and finally the actual comment itself. Because comments might contain linebreaks, each new line is replaced with a <br/> tag to match the spacing entered by the comment.

See Also

Asynchronous controllers (*http://msdn.microsoft.com/en-us/library/ee728598(v=vs.98) .aspx*)

1.18 Displaying Search Results While Typing

Problem

When you are searching for something specific, it can be difficult (or take a long time) to find it while you are trying to type the exact wording. By displaying results while the user is typing, searching for something specific becomes much easier.

Solution

Updating the existing search on the book listing page to begin displaying results immediately as the user types using *JQuery's Autocomplete plugin*.

Discussion

The Autocomplete plugin is not automatically included with MVC projects like the base JQuery library, so the first thing that needs to be done is to download the plugin by visiting *http://jquery.com/*. Two main files are required: the JavaScript file and the CSS file. Place the newly downloaded JavaScript file in the **Scripts** folder of your MVC application. The CSS file can be added to your **Content** directory.

This recipe will also introduce the use of rendering sections in a view. In the shared layout view two JavaScript files and one CSS file are automatically included on each page request. These are for the Ajax and unobtrusive Ajax and the sites main CSS file. The more content that is loaded each time, the slower the page view. So rather than automatically including JavaScript and CSS on every page when it's not needed a new **RenderSection()** will be added in the shared layout. This will allow specific views to add additional JavaScript or CSS files inside the **<head>** tags, but not require every page to add them.

Below is an updated **Views/Shared/_Layout.cshtml** with the new **RenderSection()**:

```
<!DOCTYPE html>
<html>
<head>
    <title>@ViewBag.Title</title>
    <link href="@Url.Content("~/Content/Site.css")"
            rel="stylesheet" type="text/css" />
    <script src="@Url.Content("~/Scripts/jquery-1.5.1.min.js")"
            type="text/javascript"></script>
    @RenderSection("JavaScriptAndCSS", required: false)
</head>
<body>
    <div class="page">
        <div id="header">
            <div id="title">
                <h1>My MVC Application</h1>
            </div>
            <div id="logindisplay">
                @Html.Partial("_LogOnPartial")
                [ @Html.ActionLink("English", "ChangeLanguage",
                    "Home", new { language = "en" }, null) ]
                [ @Html.ActionLink("Français", "ChangeLanguage",
                    "Home", new { language = "fr" }, null) ]
            </div>
            <div id="menucontainer">
                <ul id="menu">
                    <li>@Html.ActionLink("Home",
                        "Index", "Home")</li>
                    <li>@Html.ActionLink("About",
                        "About", "Home")</li>
                </ul>
            </div>
        </div>
```

```
            <div id="main">
                @RenderBody()
            </div>
            <div id="footer">
            </div>
        </div>
    </body>
</html>
```

The main CSS file and core JQuery files have been left in because the CSS is required on every page and the JQuery is required by a vast majority of the pages. However, the new JQuery files and the previously added unobtrusive Ajax file are not required on every page.

Now there are two ways to use the autocomplete plugin:

1. Setting the data to search in JavaScript
2. Retrieving the results via Ajax when the user types

In my experience with this plugin, I've found that the autocomplete is much faster with solution 1, because it doesn't need to request the data each time from the database. However, there is a limit to the use of this solution: only so many characters can be passed into the function, and also, rendering a large amount of JavaScript can cause the page to load slowly on the user's computer. After some trial-and-error, I've determined the magic number is around 40,000 results. If the number of results exceeds this, it's best to use option 2; otherwise, always stick to option 1 because the search is instantaneous rather than having a slight delay.

In this example, the books will be searched and we don't have more than 40,000, so option one will be used. The `BooksController` must now be updated to set a `ViewBag` variable with the list of book titles. The autocomplete function requires a JavaScript array of items, so the books will be separated with a pipe (|). Then in the view, the books will be converted to an array with the JavaScript `split()` function. When the user is finished typing in their result, they should have selected an exact match title, so this function will be updated if only 1 book is returned and the user has performed a search that will automatically redirect them to the book details page.

```
using System;
using System.Collections.Generic;
using System.Data;
using System.Data.Entity;
using System.Linq;
using System.Linq.Dynamic;
using System.Web;
using System.Web.Mvc;
using MvcApplication4.Models;
using MvcApplication4.Utils;
using PagedList;

namespace MvcApplication4.Controllers
{
```

```
public class BooksController : Controller
{
    private BookDBContext db = new BookDBContext();

    //
    // GET: /Books/
    public ActionResult Index(string sortOrder,
        string filter, string Keyword, int page = 1)
    {
        #region ViewBag Resources
        ...
        #endregion

        #region ViewBag Sort Params
        ...
        #endregion

        var books = from b in db.Books select b;

        #region Keyword Search
        if (!String.IsNullOrEmpty(Keyword))
        {
            books = books.Where(b => b.Title.ToUpper().
                Contains(Keyword.ToUpper()) ||
                b.Author.ToUpper().Contains(
                Keyword.ToUpper()));

            // Should we redirect because of only one result?
            if (books.Count() == 1)
            {
                Book book = books.First();
                return RedirectToAction("Details",
                    new { id = book.ID });
            }
        }
        ViewBag.CurrentKeyword =
            String.IsNullOrEmpty(Keyword) ? "" : Keyword;
        #endregion

        #region Filter switch
        ...
        #endregion

        books = books.OrderBy(sortOrder);

        int maxRecords = 1;
        int currentPage = page - 1;

        // Get all book titles
        ViewBag.BookTitles = FormatBooksForAutocomplete();

        return View(books.ToPagedList(currentPage,
            maxRecords));
    }
```

```
private string FormatBooksForAutocomplete()
{
    string bookTitles = String.Empty;
    var books = from b in db.Books select b;

    foreach (Book book in books)
    {
        if (bookTitles.Length > 0)
        {
            bookTitles += "|";
        }

        bookTitles += book.Title;
    }

    return bookTitles;
}

...

    }
}
```

Finally the Books/Index view needs to be updated to initialize the JQuery autocomplete. The first thing to do is to use the @section tag to include the necessary JavaScript and CSS files. Next, the previously created search textbox is updated to set an id of Key wordSearch. Finally, the JavaScript code is added at the bottom of the view to set up the autocomplete function on the search textbox. This JavaScript is intentionally added at the bottom of the view to ensure that the view is fully rendered to the user, because "blocking" the load with the JavaScript processing might require a bit of work on the user's computer to set up the data, depending on the number of results.

```
@model PagedList.IPagedList<MvcApplication4.Models.Book>

@if (IsAjax)
{
    Layout = null;
}

@section JavascriptAndCSS {
<link rel="stylesheet" href="
    @Url.Content("~/Content/jquery.autocomplete.css")"
    type="text/css" />
<script src="@Url.Content(
    "~/Scripts/jquery.unobtrusive-ajax.min.js")"
    type="text/javascript"></script>
<script type="text/javascript" src="@Url.Content(
    "~/Scripts/jquery.autocomplete.js")"></script>
}

...
```

```
@using (Html.BeginForm())
{
    @:Search: @Html.TextBox("Keyword",
                (string)ViewBag.CurrentKeyword,
                new { id = "KeywordSearch" })
    <input type="submit" value="Search" />
}

...

<script type="text/javascript">
    $(document).ready(function () {
        var data = "@ViewBag.BookTitles".split("|");
        $("#KeywordSearch").autocomplete(data);
    });
</script>
```

To implement option 2, an Ajax search, instead of passing the array of data to the autocomplete function, you would pass a URL. The URL would then need to accept a query string variable, q . This contains the user-entered search value. This would then be used to perform a search on the books that contain a partial match and would return them as a string separated by a delimiter. The JQuery documentation contains more complete examples of this, as well as other examples to update the output of the results (perhaps to include a thumbnail of the book cover).

See Also

Jquery.Autocomplete (*http://docs.jquery.com/Plugins/autocomplete*), RenderSection (*http://msdn.microsoft.com/en-us/library/gg537886(v=vs.99).aspx*)

1.19 Routing Users to a Specific Controller and Action

Problem

In today's heavily fought battles for search engine supremacy, it's quite difficult to win the race with a website address that looks like:

```
http://www.example.com/books/details?id=4.
```

Using routes, the website can look like:

```
http://www.example.com/20-recipes-for-mvc3
```

which provides much more context, both to the user and the search engine.

Solution

Use the MapRoute function from the RouteCollectionExtensions class to generate more friendly names to display content instead of numerical IDs.

Discussion

Routing is set up in MVC through the Web.config and the Global.asax.cs file. In the Web.config, the System.Web.Routing assembly is included and then used in the Global.asax.cs file to create a default routing mechanism for all controllers and actions in them. Hence when a BooksController is added, it can be accessed via the /Books URL without an extension, like in ASP.NET websites.

The following recipe will demonstrate several different useful techniques for setting up routes. The first route will allow the website to link directly to the title of the book. For example, if there is a book called *20 Recipes for Programming MVC 3*, it could be accessed directly by visiting *http://localhost/20 Recipes for Programming MVC 3*, whereas the current solution would require a more complicated URL like *http://localhost/Books/Details?id=1*.

To begin creating this route, open the Global.asax.cs file in the MVC project. A default route is created in the RegisterRoutes() function which is called from the Application_Start() function when the website first loads. The example below contains an updated RegisterRoutes function with the new route that is added with the MapRoute function:

```
using System;
using System.Collections.Generic;
using System.Linq;
using System.Web;
using System.Web.Mvc;
using System.Web.Routing;
using MvcApplication4.Models;
using System.Data.Entity;
using System.Globalization;
using System.Threading;

namespace MvcApplication4
{

    public class MvcApplication : System.Web.HttpApplication
    {
        public static void RegisterGlobalFilters(
                GlobalFilterCollection filters)
        {
            filters.Add(new HandleErrorAttribute());
        }

        public static void RegisterRoutes(RouteCollection routes)
        {
            routes.IgnoreRoute("{resource}.axd/{*pathInfo}");

            routes.MapRoute(
                "BookName", // Route name
                "{Keyword}", // URL with parameters
```

```
            new { controller = "Books", action = "Index",
            id = UrlParameter.Optional },
            new { Keyword = "\\w+" });

        routes.MapRoute(
            "Default", // Route name
            "{controller}/{action}/{id}",
            // URL with parameters
            new { controller = "Home", action = "Index",
            id = UrlParameter.Optional }
        );

    }

    protected void Application_Start()
    {
        Database.SetInitializer<BookDBContext>(
            new BookInitializer());

        AreaRegistration.RegisterAllAreas();

        RegisterGlobalFilters(GlobalFilters.Filters);
        RegisterRoutes(RouteTable.Routes);
    }

    protected void Application_AcquireRequestState(
            object sender, EventArgs e)
    {
        if (HttpContext.Current.Session != null)
        {
            CultureInfo ci =
              (CultureInfo)this.Session["CurrentLanguage"];
            if (ci == null)
            {
                ci = new CultureInfo("en");
                this.Session["CurrentLanguage"] = ci;
            }

            Thread.CurrentThread.CurrentUICulture = ci;
            Thread.CurrentThread.CurrentCulture =
              CultureInfo.CreateSpecificCulture(ci.Name);
        }
    }
  }
}
```

In the above example, the MapRoute function accepts four parameters:

1. The route name; in this case BookName.

2. The URL with any parameters; in this case, {Keyword}, which is a variable that will be used later.

3. The parameter defaults for the controller, action, and any additional variables; in this case, the default controller is Books and the default action is Index.

---

4. The constraints (e.g., variables) for the URL; in this case, the previously mentioned Keyword variable is passed to the index action in the BooksController.

The above route will take advantage of the previous change to the BooksController when a keyword is being searched: that if only one result is returned, the user will be redirected to the details page. This provides the user with the ability to enter a book title or keyword in the URL after the domain name. If only one result is returned, the user will see that book; otherwise, the user will see a search result with their keyword.

In the next example, a new route will be created that is a bit more complicated. It will extend the RouteBase class, allowing for a much more complicated route. Instead of searching for the book by the title at the end of the domain name, a subdomain will be used instead. For example, *http://mvc3book.localhost/* will return the book details for the aforementioned book *20 Recipes for Programming MVC 3*.

To allow for this, the Book model must be updated to include a new parameter called ShortName. This parameter will be used as the subdomain, and allows for the books to be searched for through the to-be-created class that extends the RouteBase class.

```
using System;
using System.Collections.Generic;
using System.Linq;
using System.Web;
using System.ComponentModel.DataAnnotations;
using MvcApplication4.Validations;

namespace MvcApplication4.Models
{
    public class Book
    {
        public int ID { get; set; }

        [Required]
        public string ShortName { get; set; }

        [Required]
        [Display(Name = "TitleDisplay", ResourceType =
                typeof(Resources.Resource1))]
        public string Title { get; set; }

        [Display(Name = "IsbnDisplay", ResourceType =
                typeof(Resources.Resource1))]
        [Required]
        [IsbnValidation]
        public string Isbn { get; set; }

        [Display(Name = "SummaryDisplay", ResourceType =
                typeof(Resources.Resource1))]
        [Required]
        public string Summary { get; set; }

        [Display(Name = "AuthorDisplay", ResourceType =
                typeof(Resources.Resource1))]
```

```
        [Required]
        public string Author { get; set; }

        [Display(Name = "ThumbnailDisplay", ResourceType =
                typeof(Resources.Resource1))]
        public string Thumbnail { get; set; }

        [Display(Name = "PriceDisplay", ResourceType =
                typeof(Resources.Resource1))]
        [Range(1, 100)]
        public double Price { get; set; }

        [Display(Name = "PublishedDisplay", ResourceType =
                typeof(Resources.Resource1))]
        [DataType(DataType.Date)]
        [Required]
        public DateTime Published { get; set; }
    }

}
```

Now a new class must be created that will contain the logic behind the new route. With the Utils folder selected, right-click and select *Add→Class*. This new class will be called BookDomainRoute.cs. The following class will retrieve the domain name from the Request.Headers for the current HttpContext. The domain name will then be split into an array by the "." operator. A bit of error checking is performed to ensure that we have a subdomain that is not *www*. Then the first piece of the subdomain, e.g., the Short Name, is used to perform a search on the books table to find the particular book. If the book is found, a new object of the class RouteData is created that sets the controller to be Books, the action to be Details, and finally the ID to be the ID of the book. If no book is found, the homepage will be displayed. In the example below, it could easily be altered to direct the user to an error page—or even to the Books/Index page with a keyword search (as in the previous example).

```
using System;
using System.Collections.Generic;
using System.Linq;
using System.Web;
using System.Web.Routing;
using System.Web.Mvc;
using MvcApplication4.Models;

namespace MvcApplication4.Utils
{
    public class BookDomainRoute : RouteBase
    {
        private BookDBContext db = new BookDBContext();

        public override RouteData GetRouteData(
                HttpContextBase httpContext)
        {
            // Get the domain name
            var url = httpContext.Request.Url.Authority;
```

```csharp
        // Split into array of parts
        var pieces = url.Split('.');

        // Ensure there is a subdomain and it's not www
        if (pieces.Length < 2 && pieces[0] != "www")
        {
            return null;
        }

        string ShortName = pieces[0];

        // Find the book by ShortName
        var books = from b in db.Books select b;
        books = books.Where(b =>
            b.ShortName.ToUpper().Contains(ShortName.ToUpper())
        );

        // Check to make sure a book was found
        if (books.Count() == 0)
        {
            return null;
        }

        // Get the first result
        Book book = books.First();

        // Set the route data
        RouteData routeData = new RouteData(this,
            new MvcRouteHandler());
        routeData.Values.Add("controller", "Books");
        routeData.Values.Add("action", "Details");
        routeData.Values.Add("id", book.ID);

        return routeData;
    }

    public override VirtualPathData GetVirtualPath(
            RequestContext requestContext,
            RouteValueDictionary values)
    {
        return null;
    }
    }
}
```

Finally the `Global.asax.cs` file must be updated again to include the newly created route. A using statement is also added to the `Utils` directory so the new routing class can be found.

```csharp
using System;
using System.Collections.Generic;
using System.Linq;
using System.Web;
using System.Web.Mvc;
using System.Web.Routing;
```

```
using MvcApplication4.Models;
using System.Data.Entity;
using System.Globalization;
using System.Threading;
using MvcApplication4.Utils;

namespace MvcApplication4
{

    public class MvcApplication : System.Web.HttpApplication
    {
        public static void RegisterGlobalFilters(
                GlobalFilterCollection filters)
        {
            filters.Add(new HandleErrorAttribute());
        }

        public static void RegisterRoutes(RouteCollection routes)
        {
            routes.IgnoreRoute("{resource}.axd/{*pathInfo}");

            routes.Add(new BookDomainRoute());

            routes.MapRoute(
                "BookName", // Route name
                "{Keyword}", // URL with parameters
                new { controller = "Books", action = "Index",
                id = UrlParameter.Optional },
                new { Keyword = "\\w+" });

            routes.MapRoute(
                "Default", // Route name
                "{controller}/{action}/{id}",
                // URL with parameters
                new { controller = "Home", action = "Index",
                id = UrlParameter.Optional }
            );

        }

        protected void Application_Start()
        {
            Database.SetInitializer<BookDBContext>(
                new BookInitializer());

            AreaRegistration.RegisterAllAreas();

            RegisterGlobalFilters(GlobalFilters.Filters);
            RegisterRoutes(RouteTable.Routes);
        }

        protected void Application_AcquireRequestState(
                object sender, EventArgs e)
        {
            if (HttpContext.Current.Session != null)
```

```
        {
            CultureInfo ci =
              (CultureInfo)this.Session["CurrentLanguage"];
            if (ci == null)
            {
                ci = new CultureInfo("en");
                this.Session["CurrentLanguage"] = ci;
            }

            Thread.CurrentThread.CurrentUICulture = ci;
            Thread.CurrentThread.CurrentCulture =
                CultureInfo.CreateSpecificCulture(ci.Name);
        }
    }
  }
}
```

The following examples contain great starts to good uses for routes. Both can be easily updated to perform other routing—for example, subdomains could be used to display a user's specific profile page, or the previously implemented multilingual recipe could be updated to use a routing class to allow URLs like en.example.com or fr.example.com to set the current language culture.

See Also

RouteCollectionExtension   (*http://msdn.microsoft.com/en-us/library/system.web.mvc .routecollectionextensions.aspx*), RouteData (*http://msdn.microsoft.com/en-us/library/ system.web.routing.routedata.aspx*)

1.20 Caching Results for Faster Page Loads

Problem

As your website grows, both in popularity as well as dynamic content, these two factors begin to slow down the average load time. Many users causes a lot of web server and database requests. A lot of data requires strong database processing power to support it. To prevent spending a lot of money of simply adding more web servers, smarter programming to reduce unnecessary database or dynamic processing requests can significantly increase the overall speed of your web application.

Solution

Implement the `OutputCacheAttribute` to cache data that doesn't change often or only changes with specific actions.

Discussion

Caching in MVC 3 is extremely easy. It's as simple as adding the following attribute above an action in a controller:

```
[OutputCache (Duration=600)]
```

This will cache the results of the view automatically for 600 seconds (or 10 minutes) and be shared for each user visiting this page. That means if you have 1,000 visitors requesting the same page in a matter of mere moments, caching the results can save on thousands of requests to the database, and lower the processing time required by IIS by simply loading an already fully processed view.

The output cache attribute looks quite simple, but when you start looking under the hood, it can be as complicated as under the hood of a car—unless you are a mechanic. This attribute allows you to define a lot about how to cache, from the duration to the location, to even adding SQL dependency. This will be explored later in this recipe.

The duration of the caching is quite simple: you tell MVC how many seconds a view should be cached for. The location is a little bit more complicated; this can be the client's browser, the server, or a combination of them. A good way to determine where the caching should be done is to analyze the data being cached. If the data being cached is shared across multiple users, it makes sense to cache this on the server. However, if it is personal data, e.g., a customized homepage, it would make sense to cache this locally on the user's browser. While caching is great, it also has its limitations. Typically the main limitation is memory; not everything can be cached on the server.

The most interesting option however, is the SQL dependency. The OutputCache allows data to be cached until it actually changes in the database. This is an extremely useful feature. Take for example, books: new books would not always be added daily, so the duration might be set to an extending caching time (24 hours, perhaps). However, what if a new book comes in before the cache expires, or if it was a slow week and no new books were added for several days? In the first situation, a new book wouldn't appear right away, which wouldn't make users too happy. In the second example, unnecessary requests are being done to the server because no new books have been added. By enabling SQL dependency, the caching will automatically be reset as soon as the books table changes; exactly the effect we want.

This is a very nice feature; in other programming languages when you need to manually control the cache, you would be required to invalidate the cache yourself as the data changes. Trust me on this one—it can be quite easy to miss a spot or two, preventing the cache from being cleared properly.

In the following example, the cache will be set up on the book listing page. By default, if you do not specify any values in the VaryByParam field, MVC 3 will automatically create one cache entry per unique variable combination. This is a pretty nice feature; however, in the book listings example, a keyword search field is accepted as one of the parameters. Since hundreds, if not thousands, of different keyword combinations could be entered, this variable should not be cached (see above warning about memory).

Instead, the params will be defined to exclude this variable. Below is an updated Book sController to enable caching on this page:

```
using System;
using System.Collections.Generic;
using System.Data;
using System.Data.Entity;
using System.Linq;
using System.Linq.Dynamic;
using System.Web;
using System.Web.Mvc;
using MvcApplication4.Models;
using MvcApplication4.Utils;
using PagedList;

namespace MvcApplication4.Controllers
{
    public class BooksController : Controller
    {
        private BookDBContext db = new BookDBContext();

        //
        // GET: /Books/
        [OutputCache(Duration=600, VaryByParam=
                "sortOrder;filter;page")]
        public ViewResult Index(string sortOrder,
                string filter, string Keyword, int page = 1)
        {
            ...

            return View(books.ToPagedList(currentPage,
                maxRecords));
        }

        ...

    }
}
```

This code only will serve a pretty good caching solution and immediately reduce the server load. This example will now be extended to include SQL dependency, as it requires a bit of setup work to begin using it. To begin, the Web.config file needs updating. Firstly, a database connection must be defined; and secondly, a caching section must be defined for the SQL dependency as follows:

```
<?xml version="1.0"?>
<configuration>
  <connectionStrings>
    <add name="ApplicationServices" connectionString=
        "data source=.\SQLEXPRESS;Integrated Security=SSPI;
        AttachDBFilename=|DataDirectory|aspnetdb.mdf;
        User Instance=true" providerName="System.Data.SqlClient"
    />
    <add name="BooksDBContext" connectionString=
        "Server=.\SQLEXPRESS;Database=
```

```
                MvcApplication4.Models.BookDBContext;
                Trusted_Connection=true" providerName=
                "System.Data.SqlClient" />
    </connectionStrings>

    ...

    <system.web>
      <caching>
        <sqlCacheDependency enabled="true" pollTime="2000">
        <databases>
          <add name = "MvcApplication4.Models.BookDBContext"
                connectionStringName = "BooksDBContext"/>
        </databases>
        </sqlCacheDependency>
      </caching>
      ...
    </system.web>

    ...
  </configuration>
```

In the above example, the pollTime variable is set to 2000 milliseconds, meaning that every 2 seconds, the cache database will be queried for changes. This should be altered as required for your needs.

Now the Global.asax.cs needs to be updated. In the Application_Start function, the SQL cache dependency must be set up, and each table that requires listening for updates must be set up with the EnableTableForNotifications function of the SqlCache DependencyAdmin class.

```
using System;
using System.Collections.Generic;
using System.Linq;
using System.Web;
using System.Web.Mvc;
using System.Web.Routing;
using MvcApplication4.Models;
using System.Data.Entity;
using System.Globalization;
using System.Threading;
using MvcApplication4.Utils;

namespace MvcApplication4
{

    public class MvcApplication : System.Web.HttpApplication
    {
        ...

        protected void Application_Start()
        {
            Database.SetInitializer<BookDBContext>(
                new BookInitializer());
```

```
            AreaRegistration.RegisterAllAreas();

            RegisterGlobalFilters(GlobalFilters.Filters);
            RegisterRoutes(RouteTable.Routes);

            String connectionString =
    System.Configuration.ConfigurationManager.ConnectionStrings
    ["BooksDBContext"].ConnectionString;
            System.Web.Caching.SqlCacheDependencyAdmin.
    EnableNotifications(connectionString);
            System.Web.Caching.SqlCacheDependencyAdmin.
    EnableTableForNotifications(connectionString, "books");
        }

        ...

    }
}
```

Next, a command line prompt is required to perform several actions to complete the SQL notifications. In Windows, perform the following steps:

```
Press Start -> Run
Type cmd and then press Enter
cd %windir%\Microsoft.NET\Framework\v4.0.30319\
aspnet_regsql.exe -S .\SQLEXPRESS -ed
   -d MvcApplication4.Models.BookDBContext -et -t books -E
```

Be sure to replace the server, database, and table name with your information. Also, if your database contains a username and password, you will need to add additional input parameters for them (-U and -P). Once the last command is run, two success messages should be displayed: one indicating successful enabling of caching on the database, and the second indicating successful enabling of caching on the specified table.

Finally, the BooksController requires a slight change to enable the SQL dependency. Also, since the application will be notified of changes, the short duration time that was previously set will be extended to use the max value for an Int32 value.

```
using System;
using System.Collections.Generic;
using System.Data;
using System.Data.Entity;
using System.Linq;
using System.Linq.Dynamic;
using System.Web;
using System.Web.Mvc;
using MvcApplication4.Models;
using MvcApplication4.Utils;
using PagedList;

namespace MvcApplication4.Controllers
{
    public class BooksController : Controller
    {
        private BookDBContext db = new BookDBContext();
```

```
//
// GET: /Books/
[OutputCache(Duration=Int32.MaxValue, SqlDependency =
    "MvcApplication4.Models.BookDBContext:books",
    VaryByParam="sortOrder,filter,page")]
public ViewResult Index(string sortOrder, string filter,
    string Keyword, int page = 1)
{
    ...

    return View(books.ToPagedList(currentPage,
        maxRecords));
}

...

    }
}
```

In previous versions of MVC, partial caching was not supported, meaning that only an entire action result could be cached. MVC 3 now supports partial caching. To enable this, you would create a child action as you did in Recipe 1.14, Submitting a Form with Ajax. The two actions in the BookCommentsController only return a *PartialView*, and both of these child actions could be cached without the need to cache the parent action. This is another great way to segregate your code and cache only the portions that don't change frequently.

See Also

OutputCacheAttribute   (*http://msdn.microsoft.com/en-us/library/system.web.mvc.out putcacheattribute.aspx*),   SqlCacheDependencyAdmin   (*http://msdn.microsoft.com/en -us/library/system.web.caching.sqlcachedependencyadmin.aspx*)

1.21 Going Further

In this book I have tried to provide you with many useful recipes that will help you in your day-to-day life to more easily accomplish recurring tasks or enhance a user's over-all experience on a website. By expanding upon the recipes involving Ajax, Mobile, jQuery, and caching and expanding these examples further, your websites should be able to take on a whole new user experience, with lightning-fast page results and ex-tremely slick, responsive user interfaces.

Every day, developers are adding new library packages to the NuGet library that can further enhance the user experience or further reduce your development time. By lev-eraging these libraries, you will have an unlimited resource of features to enhance both your website and development arsenal.

About the Author

Jamie Munro has been developing websites and web applications for over 15 years. For the past six years, Jamie has been acting as a lead developer by mentoring younger developers to enhance their web development skills.

Furthering his love of mentoring people, Jamie began his writing career on his personal blog (*http://www.endyourif.com*) back in 2009. As Jamie's blog grew in success, he turned his writing passion to books about web development.

As well as writing books, Jamie is currently in the process of starting a new website (*http://www.webistrate.com*) geared towards helping web developers further expand their experience with many online examples using MVC3, CakePHP, CodeIgniter, JQuery, Database Optimzation, and Search Engine Optimization.

Get even more for your money.

Join the O'Reilly Community, and register the O'Reilly books you own. It's free, and you'll get:

- $4.99 ebook upgrade offer
- 40% upgrade offer on O'Reilly print books
- Membership discounts on books and events
- Free lifetime updates to ebooks and videos
- Multiple ebook formats, DRM FREE
- Participation in the O'Reilly community
- Newsletters
- Account management
- 100% Satisfaction Guarantee

Signing up is easy:

1. **Go to: oreilly.com/go/register**
2. **Create an O'Reilly login.**
3. **Provide your address.**
4. **Register your books.**

Note: English-language books only

To order books online:
oreilly.com/store

For questions about products or an order:
orders@oreilly.com

To sign up to get topic-specific email announcements and/or news about upcoming books, conferences, special offers, and new technologies:
elists@oreilly.com

For technical questions about book content:
booktech@oreilly.com

To submit new book proposals to our editors:
proposals@oreilly.com

O'Reilly books are available in multiple DRM-free ebook formats. For more information:
oreilly.com/ebooks

O'REILLY®

Spreading the knowledge of innovators   oreilly.com

The information you need, when and where you need it.

With Safari Books Online, you can:

Access the contents of thousands of technology and business books

- Quickly search over 7000 books and certification guides
- Download whole books or chapters in PDF format, at no extra cost, to print or read on the go
- Copy and paste code
- Save up to 35% on O'Reilly print books
- **New!** Access mobile-friendly books directly from cell phones and mobile devices

Stay up-to-date on emerging topics before the books are published

- Get on-demand access to evolving manuscripts.
- Interact directly with authors of upcoming books

Explore thousands of hours of video on technology and design topics

- Learn from expert video tutorials
- Watch and replay recorded conference sessions

Spreading the knowledge of innovators   safari.oreilly.com